The Hat Collector & Other Flash Fiction

To Jamie

From P.W

Thanks for All Your Help!

Disclaimer & Copyright

DISCLAIMER

This book is based on some true events and places, however, it has been fictionalized, and all persons, events and places appearing in this work are fictitious. Any resemblance to real people, living or dead is entirely coincidental.

COPYRIGHT

Copyright © 2010 by Peter Worthington

All rights reserved. No part of this publication may be reproduced, distributed, or transmitted in any form or by any means, including photocopying, recording, or other electronic or mechanical methods, without the prior written permission of the publisher, except in the case of brief quotations embodied in critical reviews and certain other noncommercial uses permitted by copyright law.

For permission requests, write to the publisher, addressed "Attention: Permissions Coordinator," at the address below.

Peter Worthington
9 Byron Way

Catshill, Bromsgrove

B61 0NB

UK

Tel: 01527 879023

E-Mail: peter-worthington@sky.com

Dedication & Acknowledgements

DEDICATION AND ACKNOWLEDGEMENTS:

This book is dedicated to the real Wesley, who did show huge courage throughout his illness and times at hospital.

JOHN WESLEY WORTHINGTON: 1977-1984

It is also dedicated to my family in real life, from whom I have learned so very much. They have been ever loyal.

To my wife: Meg, from South Wales (I can hear her mother saying "her name is Margaret" from beyond the grave. She fills my life with joy and is the kindest person I know.

To my daughter: Rachel (nearly Rebecca), and her husband Andy with their two children; Rose and Ellis. I have learned so much about being a granddad through them. Rachel has often given me wisdom and encouragement.

To my son: Calvin and his wife Amy, with their baby: Max Harry.

I ought also to mention friends and associates who have greatly helped my writing. There IS a John Morgan, who served as Chair of the Board of my local housing association of which I remain a board member (2015). Bromsgrove District Housing Trust has been supportive in lots of ways; the Executive Officers always ready to befriend a weary writer.

My thanks go also to Doctors and Nurses at Great Ormond Street, and my thanks to friends in religious circles who have helped enormously.

Final mention goes to friends on FanStory, (http://www.fanstory.com), for all the great reviews and advice they have given me over the years. I have tried my best at "show not tell". Most of my short stories, poems and flash fiction have been 'tested' on my friends first.

Chapter 1 The Hat Collector And Interpreter Of Dreams

The first time I met Marcus Bailey I was not impressed. He was overweight, spotty, and had flattened short black hair with a parting. He also wore old-fashioned NHS circular wire spectacles. His clothes were retro 1960's. His enthusiasm for hats, though, was impressive. Even as a sixteen-year old he had amassed quite a collection of hats.

As a presenter with Central TV I was used to interviewing all sorts of people. I must admit, when I first heard about Marcus, I thought he would be a weirdo: and not newsworthy. My programme -Central Roundup- was looking to fill some "human interest" spots, so my camera man Josh and I were sitting in Marcus' home in Dudley in the West Midlands.

Marcus' mum served us some tea and biscuits; she was like a mother hen. "Thanks, mum, you can go now," Marcus said. I think he was eager to show us his collection, and didn't want his mum to interfere. It was not really his hats I had come to talk about, but I thought I had better get on his good side before I asked him about his other ability.

"Thank you for seeing us, Marcus", I said, "and we're grateful for your time. I'm Jesse and this is Josh. I picked up each hat in turn and examined them, feigning interest. "Our viewers will be fascinated to hear your story, Marcus. Can we record the interview as we go?" Josh lugged two black canvass bags and a portable camera across the room: not waiting for permission. He started setting up lighting.

"You're welcome, Jesse", Marcus replied, a bit hesitatingly. At first I felt that Marcus was mocking; I came to realise it's his way: he speaks slowly and politely, and I wasn't used to it.

My name was Jesse Davinsky, and it was the summer of 1986. "Our viewers will be fascinated to hear all about your hat collection and how you started", I continued, "It'd be awesome to get some personal details too." I took a deep breath. "One of your school friends," I said," contacted us originally and mentioned that you'd helped him with some nightmares that he was having; that you have a gift in interpreting dreams?" I turned and scowled at Josh who was filming, but his face was mocking.

I knew that I could be skating on thin ice, but decided to bite the bullet. I was not sure whether Marcus would go public about his "gift" but I had nothing to lose. If he wouldn't play ball, I would just run with the hat collection story.

Marcus appeared to give some thought to my question. "OK," he said, "I'm willing to be interviewed about my interpreting of dreams, as long as you give some programme time to my hat collection. I'm not a nutter. I don't want to come across as one. OK?"

I agreed, and asked Josh to record the whole interview, we would edit it all back in the studio, for airing the next evening.

To continue Marcus held up grey felt air-force beret. "This is the first hat I was given. It's what started me off," he said," my brother was in the Air Training Corps as a teenager. He joined the RAF and gave me his spare beret."

"WOW, that's interesting," I said," so this is how you started your collection?" I held the beret with a Wings insignia in my hand and twirled it.

Taking his next item he showed me a headband with feathers. Marcus explained that as a child he had been a member of the "I-Spy Club" and had received the awards from "Big Chief I-Spy from the Daily Mail because he had filled in several books. I held it carefully, looking at Josh who was doing his job.

"This is my auntie's riding helmet," Marcus said, as he held a black hat with, "they're pretty solid," he added with a tap of his knuckle. "And this is very old," Marcus said, holding a pith miner's helmet -complete with a lamp -in his hand.

"It was my father's" Marcus' mum said, her head popping around the door," he's dead now."

"Thanks, mum, why don't you get us some of your cake and more tea?" Marcus said, with an innocent look. His mother waddled out of the room, her fluffy pink slippers slapping the carpet. He gave us thumbs up. The sound of crockery came from the kitchen. Cupboard doors and drawers were opened. I noticed the kitchen door still wide open.

"We OK for sound?" Marcus said knowingly.

"Sure," Josh said, and whispered, "we can edit." Marcus winked. I felt a bit nonplussed, as if the two males had sidelined me.

"OK, Marcus," I said, "why don't you show us some more of your collection before we talk about your friend.

A grandfather clock chimed the hour. Through the bay window animals wandered below us at Dudley Zoo, just across the road.

"Josh," I said, "try and get some of the zoo in the shot."

With pride he held up a motorcycle helmet with the insignia of the Automobile Association. "The helmet is my dad's. He was a patrolman with the AA, and always saluted AA members. He doesn't have his motorbike and sidecar now, he has a mini-van." His 'World-Famous Hat Collection' filled every corner of his parents' lounge, plastic stacking boxes rising to the ceiling. His mum peeking around the door - noticing me looking at the boxes - said: "He's got more boxes in his bedroom. I don't know where he gets it from: it must be on his dad's side of the family. "There were bonnets, bowlers, army helmets, trilbies, top hats and a host of others.

Marcus' mum, a jolly forty-plus lady clad in blue-chequered apron, returned. She carried a flowery-patterned tray, with brown tea-pot, silver milk jug and sugar bowl. In the centre of a mahogany table she placed the tray with a cake display. As I balanced the bone china cup and plate, I smiled a thank-you to her. She reminded me of a hospital matron: always busy and finding things to do. Josh too was at his politest, placing his equipment beside a side-board, he sat at a dining-room table; saying nothing.

"Thanks, mum, you can go now," Marcus announced, fidgeting. His mum went into the kitchen, humming a tune.

Once I felt that Marcus had shown us what he wanted to, I asked him to tell us a bit about his ability to interpret dreams, when it started and what sort of help he gave, without breaking any confidences.

He began by telling us about his school friend, the one who had contacted Central Newsroom.
"My friend Alan," Marcus said," no names right? "Josh and I nodded.
"Well he was sitting next to me in an IT class, and appeared worried about something; really worried." Marcus said," I mean who has bags under their eyes at our age?"
I wasn't sure who the "OUR" was, I was some years older than Marcus and had known weary nights, tossing and turning.
"Anyway I asked him 'what's the problem, dude?' We guys aren't so talkative about feelings n' stuff. But I guess he was desperate, so he opened up." Marcus said. "He'd been having the same nightmare for weeks. Two cats would fight in the house, a black one and a white one. The white cat would win the fights, despite both being hurt, and the black cat limped down the garden path, looking back towards the front door and then slinks away."
"Hey, this sounds awesome," Josh interrupted, zooming in with his Video Camera.

"Well I thought about it a few minutes and then it hit me, I felt like a light bulb came on in my head, " Marcus said," I asked him if he had a brother. Yes he did. Did they get on? Well they used to, but lately had been having arguments. Then I said, with my hand on his shoulder, 'What you're dreaming about is your home situation. The cats are you and your brother. You're really upset about the rows; worried that one day he might leave home. You feel sad about this, and would like the fights to stop."

It sounded so simple, but what Marcus told his friend gave him answers. He and his brother talked about some of the problems they were having, and he never had that nightmare again. Marcus described other people, neighbours, friends of his mum, and even two school-teachers that he had helped by reading their dreams.

"I think it's a gift," his mother called from the kitchen.

I thanked Marcus once again for his time, and we packed our kit into my Central TV car. Josh and I headed back to Birmingham. I was not sure what our viewers would think about it all, but decided we would edit, broadcast and see what happened. The interview was aired that evening as a ten-minute focus during the Central Roundup. The producer had told me that she was going out on a limb for me, and just hoped that we didn't get crank calls. I could use my figure, long blonde hair and blue eyes with male producers, but Alison played hard-ball.

I did not give the programme much thought on the next day as I was busy in the city, and we were getting ready for the Golf Tournament on Sunday. The Classic could be a ratings bonus. When I arrived at the Central offices in Broad Street, the producer's PA, Jenny, said, "You've a message from Carlos Ortiz." I knew of Ortiz, he was over here for the Classic Tournament at the Belfry. His form had dipped the last few matches, but he was still a contender to win.

I looked at the scribbled message on a yellow stick-it note stuck to my PC monitor. "Please call me, Carlos Ortiz; with a mobile number." He had given his mobile number! I could not believe that I had the private mobile number of a golfing celebrity: this could open mega doors, I thought. Carefully pressing the number keys on my mobile, a mechanical voice said: "please leave a message after the beep." I left a message using my poshest voice. I was lifting a beaker of ice-chilled water from the dispenser to my lips when my phone rang. Queens 'all we need is radio gaga' bouncing off the walls, as my phone vibrated and fell to the floor. Laughs circulated the office. Relieved that my phone was OK and still ringing; I pressed 'Talk' and listened to the Spanish voice, sticking my tongue out at the office jokers. He wanted to meet Marcus, and would meet any expenses and any terms and conditions we made, subject to his PR agreeing.

I ran up the spiraling metal stairs and knocked on Alison's open door; a part glazed wooden door, with 'PRODUCER' on it. She practiced an 'open door' ethos: If it was open, knock and enter. But you'd better be sure you needed to.
"Hey guess what?" I said, and told her the news. Her brow furrowed. We talked things over a while - it was really me talking breathlessly - and her listening. After we had talked some more Alison pressed a number on her desk intercom, putting our legal on speakerphone.
"I think we can get some mileage out of this," Alison said, drinking from her Aston Villa mug, recapping for the benefit of her audience.
"I think we can get Carlos to interview for us, and feature it as part of our Golf coverage on Sunday." I said, my hands feeling clammy.
"I agree," Alison said. "What about confidentiality, regarding his meeting with 'the dream-reader', Mike?"

A voice over the speakerphone replied, "It shouldn't be a problem if we agree that any conversations Ortiz has with Marcus will be private.... What about his agent?"

"If Jesse takes a contract and terms & conditions with her, Carlos can talk with his agent." Alison said. "...OK?"

The voice on speakerphone said, "Agreed", and I nodded.

"Ok", she said, "Sports are covering mainly The Classic Tournament, but why don't you walk with Carlos? Remember, though, that the main issue is confidentiality. Whatever conversations Ortiz made with Marcus would be private. Got that? Only tell the viewers what Ortiz says you can; his PR guy will be there so it's cool."

I phoned and made arrangements with Marcus. At 10.00 Sunday morning I turned left opposite Dudley Zoo, some families were going through the turnstiles, and peeped our horn outside Marcus' home. He strolled down the garden path whistling. His mum chased after him, "your sandwiches," she called out as he opened the gate.

I told yam, mum, I don't need 'me," he said over his shoulder.

Mum waved from the gate, clutching a Betterware box. The broadcast crew in the back we set off for The Belfry. We joined the M5 at Oldbury, took the M6 later and went onto the M42. As we pulled up outside the Belfry Hotel & Country Club I could tell that Marcus was nervous, but was enjoying the experience anyway.

A porter with purple jacket met us and took us through reception. The broadcast crew wandered off to find the Sports crew. The legend that was Carlos Ortiz was having coffee in the restaurant/bar. Coffee and breakfast smells were in the air.

The Tournament started at 2pm for a knockout stage, but as Carlos was already ranked and qualified, he would not play a round until Monday.

I recognised Carlos immediately. His jet black hair, handsome Adonis-like features, he was the face used by mega sponsors; household names, probably disappointed at his lack of success lately.

My heels clicked on the marble-tile floor, Marcus' eyes roamed to and 'fro. I was pleasantly surprised that he didn't seem fazed by the luxurious setting. His hair was no longer flat and parted, but sleek and gelled: he looked at home. A smartly-attired man at his table stood to welcome us: obviously his agent. I stretched my right hand forwards, "Hello, my name is Jesse Davinsky, from Central TV, and this young man is Marcus Bailey." I said shaking his hand. "Please sit down. John could you get a waiter?" he addressed to the other guest. Carlos spoke with a slight accent, but his English was easily understood. "Please call me, Carlos", he answered, showing a warm smile with sparkling white teeth as we shook hands. "Please sit down". The waiter took our orders, as we exchanged a few more pleasantries about the weather, the tournament, news generally. Marcus happily spread marmalade on his croissants and gazed around. Other celebrities were eating.

Suddenly Marcus stopped eating and asked, "Do you have a spare hat, Mr. Ortiz?" We all stopped eating. John raised his eye-brows at me. "Do you have a hat, Mr. Ortiz?" I nearly choked. Clearly Carlos was pensive, but then, after seconds he brightened and laughed, relaxing us all.

"The World-Famous Hat Collection needs another?" Carlos asked, clapping Marcus on the back. He waved the waiter to our table, with a commanding air. The waiter returned after some minutes with a plastic carrier bag with Classic Tournament Logos. Placing the presents before Marcus Carlos said, "They're yours." Inside were a Belfry cap and a Classic Golf Tournament 1986 cap. Marcus was overjoyed.

Carlos and I chatted for a while about the Tournament and our extra sports coverage, which would be a profile of Golfing Star coverage, fixing terms and times for interviews. His agent signed two copies of the contract and our T & C's. Carefully folding my copy, I touched Marcus' shoulder, then John and I left the table; so that he and Marcus could get down to the personal reason for Carlos' call.

I returned after an hour and could see that Carlos had been tearful. Marcus sat with his arm around his shoulder. It appeared they had reached a breakthrough. I knew that I could not pry; not easy for a reporter. The Tournament was a great success, and even though Carlos did not win, he came a good second; pundits said he was playing better than ever. The broadcast van was going to stop for several days, so Marcus and I took a taxi. Comfortable in the back seat I did catch him looking at my legs. I felt strangely pleased: like when workers wolf-whistle me in the street. I put it down to his hormones.

In the ride home Marcus told me that he had helped Carlos to understand his dream and why he was struggling in his golf. He was also going to get Marcus an item he had wanted for years, Marilyn Monroe's beret from "Some like it hot". Sure enough a few months later Marcus phoned me to say it had arrived.

Two years passed and I came across Marcus at an Agricultural Show near to Malvern. I knew it was his stall straight away as a sign on a mobile caravan said: "The World Famous Hat Collection…….your dreams read inside". I knocked on the door and he appeared. He leaped down the steps and hugged me with, "Hey, Jesse! How are you?" I didn't mind the hug. He had changed quite a lot. His spots had gone, he had lost some weight, but he still had no fashion sense. Over khaki brown trousers he wore a baggy jumper. On his feet he had sandals.

I could see that some of his collection was displayed "NOT FOR SALE" in a clear cabinet. Some hats he was selling retail with price labels attached. "It's lovely to see you again, Marcus", I announced, extending my hand. "Looks like you're doing okay."

He told me that he was studying fashion at Dudley College, but was also doing shows. I asked him how the dream-reading was progressing, and he seemed a bit embarrassed.

"Err; I only take people's details now, as some lady's husband didn't like her talking to me in the caravan. Also without somebody minding my stall I could lose all my stock while I'm in the mobile." I laughed but could imagine jealous husbands where Marcus was concerned: he was becoming a handsome young man; I saw the wisdom of his change of method about his stock. "Have you had any more celebrities asking for help?" I asked Marcus. Secretly I hoped there was another story.
"Well I did have a lady in Miami ring me a few weeks ago, but I just could not afford to go and see her. Carlos Ortiz had told her about me."

When Marcus told me her name I was flabbergasted. She was one of the world's most famous fashion designers.
"Let me give her a call, Marcus, maybe I can help." We agreed that I would do that the next day. I gave him a peck on the cheek and he blushed. I felt hot as I walked away. After a few calls to Sandra Louise Gordon, spending time talking with PA's' secretaries and agents, I finally tracked her down to her San Francisco boutique. "Ms. Gordon," I assured her," Marcus would love to

meet you, and wants to see you." I said. Everyone in my office held their breath. "My office can make the arrangements if we can agree an interview." After a pause she agreed. Putting the phone down, I raised my fist raised in the air, and shouted "Yeah!" Staff whistled and cheered. Sandra Louise Gordon did not do interviews. Even at her fashion exhibitions - attended by stars and fashion gurus- she only spoke fashion.

Alison quieted the crowd gathering around me, and said, "that's brilliant, Jesse, well done. Step into my office and we can go over our plan." Suddenly it was 'her' plan? Sandra's office faxed details of her proposal, which included First Class airfare for Marcus and me, and most importantly, I could interview her, and the tape - once her people had edited it - could be syndicated worldwide. After much persuasion Marcus' mum agreed that he could go across the world with me; the clincher being that the SLG fashion house experience would be a massive step-up in his career. God, I thought: 'I am twenty-six and he is eighteen; what did she think I was going to do - run off with him? I assured her that Marcus' safety was my priority,

The taxi collected me from Central's offices, and then we picked up Marcus. He placed a small suitcase in the boot and slung in his rucksack as a Flight Bag.
"Passport?" I asked.
"Yes, Jesse." Marcus replied with a goofy salute. We chatted excitedly on the back seat, like two schoolchildren, as the black taxi sped along the motorways. Marcus told me he had never flown before: his only trip abroad had been a school trip to France from Dover to Calais on the hovercraft.
"Don't worry, Marcus, I'll look after you," I felt goose-bumps unable to discern why I was so excited.
"Thanks," he said, as we pulled into the drop-off zone, quickly unloading our luggage.

Marcus had never flown before, so was very excited. Birmingham International was a thriving airport with lots to see. At the AirFrance check-in, two girls with smart suits and sparkling smiles greeted us. Our cases chugged across the conveyor, I swung my hand-luggage over my shoulder; Marcus his rucksack over his. Of course Marcus bought a sombrero in Duty Free. He placed it on his head and snapped his fingers, twirling as a matador. "OK," I thought," what have you done with the real Marcus Bailey?" I chuckled as he posed for photos. Passers-by laughed with us: I think they assumed we were a couple.

On board the Airbus we settled into conversation, relaxing in the First Class comfort of a luxurious double seat - a new innovation from the Airline. Marcus looked through his window as the plane careered down the runway with a roar of its engines. Seeing the tarmac left behind I was surprised how easily I could chat to Marcus: It was like we were really close friends.

Tearing wrappers from his breakfast tray items Marcus munched and swallowed while I typed. He settled into the in-flight movie while I worked on my laptop. I was preparing some interview questions for Sandra Louise, as she NEVER gave interviews and had promised me one as part of our deal. She had also offered to pay First Class fares for us both, but I negotiated terms to syndicate our interview and use the best crew available at her expense. During the flight Marcus leg brushed against mine, but I didn't mind. He also fell asleep and leaned slightly on me, but I figured he was the star not me. When he woke up he was obviously embarrassed and apologised. "It's like the seats for couples in the cinema," I said, feeling the colour rise to my cheeks. "Yeah, that's cool," Marcus responded. He looked like he had been mulling something over. "Oh… I got to go somewhere … Stay here."

Taking a big breath Marcus went to the preparation area. Despite protestation at first they relented when Marcus explained his plan. One took him forward and knocked on the Flight Deck's door. The stewardesses were giggling and after ten long minutes, I could see by the huge grin on his face that Marcus had got what he wanted. He held a loft a dark navy AirFrance Captain's hat and took a bow as I clapped. It was a spare. They must have heard about their passenger.

"It's his spare," Marcus said, "And he let me sit next to him and explained the controls."

In arrivals a chauffeur liveried with 'Ramada Inn' uniform held a placard with MARCUS BAILEY in bold print, I steered us towards him, Marcus pushing our luggage trolley. He shook the driver's hand like he was a long-lost friend, which put a smile on his face. My companion had an ability to make people comfortable; he was definitely growing on me. Climbing into the sleek black Limousine Marcus said, "Wow!", and examined the arm-rests, phone, TV, and fax machine in the rear. As we passed huge hoardings Marcus pointed at some saying, "Look at that, Jesse!" He repeated, "Awesome" and "Epic" but I was waiting for the question I knew was coming as we pulled up at the hotel.

"Do you have a spare chauffeur hat?" he asked the driver. He replied that he didn't but if Marcus asked the Concierge he would obtain one. He also winked and told Marcus that they could get him anything. I don't think he understood, and I was glad that I didn't have to explain "the escort business".

Our rooms were plush and had everything, including bar, Jacuzzi, cable TV and lots of freebies. We were in adjacent identical rooms, the only challenge being Marcus getting used to having no key. He inserted a hotel swipe card several times until the keypad blinked with green lights. SLG Fashion was collecting us from our hotel that evening to show us the sights of San Francisco. We were meeting Sandra Louise herself for late dinner at 9pm. She had arranged a brief tour, so after we freshened up we sat in the lounge waiting for the Limo. I could smell his soap. He had made an effort with his attire, with white shirt and black Wrangler jeans.

Both Marcus and I were impressed with China Town, the Golden gate bridge, the Trolley-rides and the epic harbor views. I don't know why but I was feeling a bit emotional. Maybe it was the romantic setting. "Pull yourself together, girl", I thought.

After the limo dropped us off at Madame Wong's, a world famous Chinese restaurant. Sandra Louise was already seated and waved to us as we entered. The table was a large round revolving table in the centre, with settings around. There were place settings for six, so I reasoned that Sandra Louise had invited other guests. Throughout the meal, which started at 20.55 and finished at 1.05 the next day, the waiters brought about 50 courses. Marcus looked at me before he ate anything, as some food was dished onto our plates, and other dishes were eaten in the hand and dipped in various sauces. Sandra Louise and Marcus were talking intermittently throughout the evening, sometimes looking serious, other times laughing.

Three guests arrived at about 23.00; I recognised one as being a leading film producer, but the others I didn't know. They were introduced, more to Marcus than to me; the pastor of a huge Baptist church and TV preacher, and the owner of one of the world's largest chain of Department stores.

The Baptist pastor and Marcus were occupied for the most of the evening once they started talking. I could hear snippets about: Joseph; Moses; Daniel; Ezekiel; Mary & Joseph; Peter; and Paul. I assumed that all of these people had some involvement in dreams or dream-reading, so I left them to it while I talked with Sandra Louise between mouthfuls. When we finally shook hands, the Baptist pastor had promised Marcus his Mortar-board hat from Theological Seminary, JD Parker of Parkhurst properties had promised a hard-hat from his construction site, and we had arranged a meeting with Sandra Louise at her design studio midday.

In the Limo drive back to the hotel, though I was knackered, I was interested to hear what our dream-reader had made of the night. He did not want to go into any detail, but he assured me that Sandra Louise now understood her dreams, what camels and ships meant, and that her latest fashion show would be amazing. I was becoming increasingly fascinated by my young friend.

I was eating breakfast in my PJ's in my room later that day, when I heard a knock. I thought it may be room service, so I asked them to come in. It was Marcus, fresh out of the Jacuzzi and wrapped in a Ramada Inn white robe. I adjusted my PJ top, and asked him to take a seat, and

You want some toast, Marcus?"
"No thanks. You want to take a dip?" he asked.
"I have lots of work to do on my laptop, and some phone calls to make, but I'll join you in half an hour. Okay?"
"Great" he said, looking like the cat that got the cream.

Marcus swam towards me, his hair wet and a bit tossed about. Without his 1960's cords and jumper, he looked cool. In fact he looked handsome as he swam towards me. I was wearing my one-piece black number, very modest. He lifted me by my arms gently easing me into the pool. I was feeling quite heady. It had been years since I had been lifted by a man. A man! What was I thinking? Marcus was a good eight years younger than me. He was a boy! I suddenly had a mental image of his mother and ducked my head under the water. We swam and frolicked in the pool for about an hour, enjoying the California sunshine and the coolness of the water.

When Marcus' hair was wet and a bit tossed about, he didn't seem as nerdy. Without his 1960's cords and jumper, he looked cool. In fact he looked handsome as we swam towards me. I was wearing my one-piece black number, very modest. He lifted me by my arms and gently eased me into the pool. I was feeling quite heady. It had been years since I had been lifted by a man. A man! What was I thinking? Marcus was a good eight years younger than me. He was a boy! I suddenly had a mental image of his mother and ducked my head under the water. We swam and frolicked in the pool for about an hour, enjoying the California sunshine and the coolness of the water.

I don't know whether Sandra Louise or the hotel had laid on some clothes for Marcus, but he did look very different later that morning. He had Levi jeans, white open-necked shirt and navy jacket. He had long ago ditched his NHS specs for designer glasses. I was in my floral Laura Ashley print dress and pumps. In the car to SLG design studio, Marcus touched my hand once affectionately. I felt a tingle. What was happening? I was a hard-nosed TV journalist and presenter, my job was my life.

At SLG we were shown around the studio, introduced to all Sandra's people, and shown the range for the next fashion show in Paris. Marcus, of course, was eager to know what hats were being used, and where the accessories were from. After lunch there was a film shoot, which was the one that Central TV would own and syndicate. I interviewed Sandra Louise Gordon in a made-up lounge setting. I was the first to be granted this privilege. Many said that it was the best and frankest interview that had ever been recorded. When I phoned my boss, Alison, after the interview I could not believe the praise!

On the flight home Marcus and I mainly slept. This time I rested my head on his chest. He didn't seem to mind. We went through customs at Birmingham and I gave Marcus a hug as we parted. Some weeks after our trip to San Francisco I had a call from Marcus. JD Parker of Parkhurst properties had given him free retail concessions with staff in all his department stores and in addition was leasing him a large retail shop in Stratford upon Avon for his unique collection. The World Famous Hat Collection was going global.

With my personal embossed invite I attended the official opening in Stratford. Marcus has arranged the shop so that his 'World Famous Hat Collection' was displayed in cabinets around the area, but the centre was a relaxing lounge area. There were free non-alcoholic drinks for anyone who wanted to look around or sit and chat. Marcus asked me to take a seat in the lounge settee and talk. I gradually opened up about a dream I had been having since a teenager. I would often wake up covered in perspiration. Marcus explained that many times either experience we have had, even on that day, would trigger some emotion or memory.
As we chatted more he came over and kissed me on my lips. "I dream about you every night", he said.
"Yes, me too" I replied nervously.

Later that evening I was relaxed in his arms in the pull-down bed on his house-boat. The rise and fall of the Avon's waters helped to make the moment even more sensual.

"You realise that if we get married, I'll have to get a hat, "Marcus whispered into my ear.

"Is that a question?" I asked? "If it is, the answer is YES!"

Chapter 2 The Great Escape Plan

THE GREAT ESCAPE PLAN

Green space spreads out as far as the hospital drive-way and gates. Oak trees and some leafy bushes cast shadows.

"They'll give good cover", I reason.

Already I am planning my escape.

The boredom is driving me nuts. I have been here ten days, two hundred and forty hours, or 14,400 minutes. Observed every second like a caged animal. I was set free, yet locked up. Friends don't visit, family won't. I have my own room, meals three times a day, some recreation and TV.

Saint Clements, whoever he was, is framed in an oil-painting in the lounge. The hospital bears his name. Underneath his portrait is the text: "*The Truth will set you free.*" It wouldn't be the truth setting ME free; it would be my personal escape plan!

"Not guilty by reason of Insanity". My defense lawyer suggested my plea. What a crock of turd! I am no more insane than the next man. Obviously not the next man here: as he IS a nutter! Every night I hear him banging his head on his wall. Maybe it's his idea of fun? Some really odd people walk around here. None of the doctors or staff wear white coats, so it's a laugh to guess who is "normal".

The best fun is when I mess with the psychiatrist's head. We play "next word" games, and I always answer with a weird association. The pictures he shows me on his desk look the same to me, "spiders", I say. I know what he's after. They want to "diagnose my condition". They want to start "therapy". I would like to "do some therapy" on them, but that's what got me here. "Temper; temper!"

My evening meal of ham salad is half-eaten on my desk. I am working in the dark on my "escape plan". The CCTV monitors with infra-red will record me writing. Room search will find some duff poems I have written. The real notes are in a plastic bag inside a banana in the fridge. The male nurse, who is on the night-shift, found my "suicide" note in the toilet cistern, as I knew he would. What a panic that caused! Ha-ha. My plan is precise, each step numbered logically. My plan is daring. Some would even say, "It's insane", so I may prove them right.

Each night I've been completing:-

Step One: Loosen putty around window frame. I set myself two hours per night for four nights. Eight hours, or 480 minutes of etching away with the plastic knife from my dinner tray, ensuring there is no evidence. Then follows:-

Step Two: (which is tasked for Saturday evening at 20.30, when everybody is doped up with pills) .Remove window pane and place under bed.

Step Three: Tie bed sheets around toilet and tug to check safety, lower sheets out of the window. Apply black shoe polish to face in a striped-fashion.

Step Four: (to be accomplished quietly and without injury to self) Climb slowly down sheet, dropping stealthily to ground.

Step Five: using zigzag motion and crouching periodically, hurry towards the trees and bushes. (This should be completed by 20.40 or the mission is aborted)

Step Six: using cover and darkness, approach the main gates and scale the iron railings. (Take care not to snare trousers on railings or drop down too heavily, thereby causing pain and/or noise)

Step Seven: Walk calmly towards the village. Once arrived at bus stop wait without causing suspicion. (This must be accomplished by 20.50 for bus arrival or plan has failed)

Step Eight: Board bus, pay driver £1.50 fare for Morrison's' Roundabout.

Step Nine: ETA 21.20 Refer to map and locations, and find X spot.

Step Ten: Apocalypse! Attack everyone in sight. (Use: kicking, biting, punching - until zone is clear and task is complete.)

Chapter 3 Are You Going To San Francisco?

The cell was eight feet wide. A stained and cracked ceramic sink stood against the wall adjacent to the filthy toilet which had no seat. My cell door was solid steel with a sliding hatch for food and a small "peep-hole". Drawings, rude limericks, names and dates were etched into the crumbling wall above my mattress. The tiny window was too high to look out of without a climb. "Lights out" crackled loudly through the speaker above the door. Pulling the string cord, I turned out the naked light bulb and was immersed in an inky blackness, left in the dark with my thoughts. Sounds faded as the night wore on.

Adjusting to the long lonely nights in Alcatraz's correctional facility took most inmates a few weeks or months. The cons were hard-timers, mainly lifers, most needing a maximum security detention due to the violence of their crimes. I was there, not because of any murder or rape, but to ensure I remained incarcerated. I had escaped seven times in five years, so The Rock was regarded essential for my continued rehabilitation, or so the warden had said.

"You know why you are here, Scott? A judge and jury found you guilty of fraud, and you must serve your sentence in full," so detailed the warden, a balding portly man called Blake. Sweating profusely, despite the cold, he added, "There will be no escape from here, and any attempt will add more years to your sentence."

With my humblest nod and expressions of remorse, I said, "Yes, sir. I appreciate that. Thank you, Warden."

I hurriedly scanned his desk, filing cabinets, waste bins and shelves, for anything I could use. Distracting him subtly by switching my vision to his window, I pocketed a metal twelve inch ruler. Maybe I could sharpen it later. It would be a handy weapon.

"It's no use gazing out of the window. During your two hours yard exercise you'll be watched by the guards in the wall towers. I repeat. There will be NO escape. Am I clear?"

"Yes, Sir. Of course, Sir. Sorry sir."

Walking around the grey dirt yard for two hours a day was our exercise. The wind whipped water from the ocean waves and hit our faces like hard rain. Giving an occasional nod to inmates and plunging my hands into my pockets, I walked the rectangular perimeter. Conversations were seldom long to avoid suspicious looks from the armed guards in the towers on the cold cement walls.

My opportunity was growing, however, during the weekly Sunday service in the prison chapel. I used any skills I had or learned to generate sympathy and conversation. The Methodist minister was eager to listen to my tale of woe. An appointment was made for a meeting in the library later that week.

Inmates felt the separation and isolation that prison life created. We were meant to regret being there: on Alcatraz island life behind bars was punishment not rehabilitation. Boisterous sea waves crashed against the bleak rocks reminding any of the futility of escape. Attempting escape many had drowned, died of hypothermia, been eaten by sharks, or been driven crushingly onto the rocks.

"Good morning, number 17501, how are you feeling this afternoon? This is my last appointment this week," the minister prompted sympathetically.

"Call me, Scott, please," I suggested. I knew, of course, that mine was the last interview. It was part of my plan.

"Certainly, Scott it is then. Are you still feeling homesick and depressed?"

Feigning tears and brokenness I shook and sobbed, hoping that the minister was tactile and I had guessed correctly about his sexuality. My ruse worked, the clergyman came to place a tender hand upon my shoulder. Gazing upwards into his face I placed my hand upon his, watching for a response.

"You'll get used to it, Scott. It will get easier."

"But I miss my boyfriend so terribly. When I was transferred here I was devastated," I lied.

I started to sob again, hoping that it would encourage him. Sure enough he put both arms around me and gave me a hug. Seizing my moment I turned my face towards his and kissed him on the lips. I met resistance at first, but soon found the kiss being returned, but he seemed to panic.

"No, we can't!" he pleaded.

"Please, I need you. Let's go into the small office. I want you."

In the security and privacy of the office, the minister lost all inhibition as we removed each other's clothes. After a short time of caressing and foreplay I grabbed him and using strips of cloth I had secreted days before, I placed a gag over his mouth and tied his hands and feet. The minister sobbed, shaking, as I tied him to a table leg and donned his clothes. A near perfect fit.

I walked quickly from the library to the hall and guard room, pulling the collar of the Methodist minister's overcoat to cover my face. Blowing into my hands my body language expressed the cold as I avoided eye-contact with the uniformed guard. Solid steel locks clunked together as the doors opened and I was on the outside of the prison, braced against the cold wind. Carefully I descended the rocky steps down to the motor-boat docked and waiting for me.

Nervously I stepped into the boat as it rose and fell with the current. Powering the diesel motor the ferryman moved across the waves towards my freedom. Every second as the craft moved over the water I focused on the distant shore, which was getting closer and closer.

Sirens sounded on The Rock. I shrugged my shoulders towards the boat's owner.

"Don't ask me, my son. I was on God's work and have seen no trouble," I explained to the man as we slowed up. Placated, he opened the throttle again, and we sped towards the jetty.

Disembarking the boat I wished the boatman "God speed", and quickly made my way towards the San Francisco bus station. My plan was to catch the first bus leaving the terminus and get to any place. I knew that as a fraudster and con-man I would try again, hopefully I would not be caught. The cells were getting smaller.

Chapter 4 A Dining Out Experience

I ate a worm. Not sliced or dissected, I just opened wide and swallowed it whole. The long soft body wriggled and squirmed. It suffocated in my throat.

I had been thinking about eating a worm for days. They looked so appetising. Needing to wait until the garden was deserted, I bode my time. I was dining alone.

It's a shame 600 million years of existence met its match. Without any teeth I needed something easily chewable. Worms can live for 10 years. Mine is dead now. The wriggling has stopped. It was a tough little thing. It put up a fight.

Contrary to what some think, worms have hairs, are strong and can live underground in freezing weather. They are most vulnerable when they pop their heads up or slither around the soil. At least one will slither no more. Not in my back-yard. My worm tasted a bit salty.

Preening my black and white feathers I am going to look for another one before the blackbird comes back!

Chapter 5 Lost And Found

They left me. My family had packed belongings into a white van and gone. As I watched the vehicle disappear around my street corner I felt sad. Chasing after them would be pointless. I could never keep up.

Over the past few weeks there had been secret meetings. I heard the hushed talk; I never imagined they would up stakes and leave me alone. So here I was, outside my home for five years, sitting alone. I decided I would follow them.

Food was easy to come by. Discarded burgers, chips left on a wall, yoghurt in a bin. I would survive. Being so young I had to watch my step in the moonlit streets. Street lights illumined dark shadows as I trudged on.

The next day the sun was hot on my back, but I kept walking. Ignoring the aches in my joints and the soreness of my feet I pressed on. Passing the familiar sights of the church and smells of the Indian takeaway the miles wore on. Recognising the traffic island in the high street, I rushed over quickly. Traffic was building now.

I dodged between the pedestrians, crossing the road to the park. It was one of my favourite places to play. I had no time today. Using my best instincts, drawing upon scant memories of overheard mutterings, I crossed the road by the school.
Yes! The van was there.

Licking my paws and stroking my whiskers I made my way to our new home.

Chapter 6 A Miracle Child

"Did you see that?" Mary called out with astonishment, "our child just moved his baby-rattle without touching it!"

Coming into the main house I said, "Na - it must have rolled with gravity or he nudged it."

Undeterred, my partner repeated with firmness: "I'm telling you that he moved that toy by looking at it ... it went flying into his hand." Not for the first time I found myself biting my tongue: after all I had married her as a pregnant teenager, against all advice, but maybe she was right to say the child was special.

The happenings of the past few years had been traumatic enough - but now that we had escaped those who were trying to kill us - I was glad to be home. News of slaughtered babies and infants had reached our ears as we travelled from town to town. I worked by the roadside, at markets or doing work for caravan owners. The first three years of our married life was a roller-coaster - hiding in a foreign country, learning a different language. We had no home of our own.

Back in my home town family and friends visited us, offering their congratulations: different to his birth when total strangers had turned up. Some brought presents, but it was a massive intrusion: as a new family we needed our space. My workshop was once more a centre of commerce: taking orders and studying designs and wood prices. Our first son, followed by two brothers and two sisters, became helpful, but there was always a "mystical" look on his face. Whilst he helped - in between his schooling - I got the sense that he didn't fit in.

One day, on a journey we were forced to make to the capital, I was horrified to find that he had gone missing. Assuming he was walking with his cousins it was into the third morning that we realised he wasn't with the caravan. Making our apologies we hastened back to the city to start our search. Reluctant to involve the military my wife and I looked up and down the streets until Mary said, "let's look in the temple". Reluctantly I agreed, bribing the guards to allow us through the ornate doors. Imagine my surprise when I saw him, surrounded by a circle of grown-ups, holding them spell-bound with his dialogue.

On the way home a silence dominated the atmosphere. We arrived home days after our friends - to subtle hints about our ability as parents. Mary was upset that we were being judged, our son placating her. "It's not your fault, Mum. You know I have a mission. I get focused on that sometimes."

When I heard what he had said I was livid! "Mission indeed - listen, Mary, you must stop taking his side. I feel like an outsider sometimes."

During his teens stories followed our first child. Tales of the bereaved comforted, the mentally ill given hope, and the sick being healed. As he was busy in my business, and my health was failing, I didn't like to question his attitude. Teachers in the local assembly had visited me over the years to take a look at the "odd child". Some were impressed and went away full of praise for him, others were very critical.

As my illness became more serious, and I knew that I wouldn't have long, I asked him to talk with me privately.

"Son, your brothers have married, and one of your sisters is engaged. I want you to promise me something"

"Okay, Dad. If it's something I can do, I will give you my word."

"I want you to promise that you will look after your mother. When I am gone, she will need you to be the man. I know one day you might get married, but please assure me that your mum will live with you."

"Dad, I promise whatever is in my power to do, I will do for mum. I will ensure that she is looked after."

I sensed that he would keep his word. I could die at peace.

Chapter 7 Behind The Green Door

The green-painted door was unusually locked with a chain and padlock. Nothing on the holiday brochure suggested we couldn't have access to the rooms of the cottage, so I was annoyed that one feature was hidden. I tested the strength of the chain, deciding the door hid something. With my ear pressed against the cold wooden door I could hear something moving inside, like a scratching noise.

'Was somebody or something trapped inside?' I thought.

The previous night my wife and I had not slept. It was always the same the night before a holiday: the anticipation kept us tossing and turning. Throwing off the duvet Megan stretched, turned off the alarm - which had proved unnecessary - and sat on the bed.

"Come on, Peter, we may as well finish packing and set off," she said, pushing me gently.

"OK. Get the kettle on and I'll shave," I yawned.

An open case sat on the settee as Meg placed in a few more articles. I shoved my shaving gear, mobile charger, kindle and tablets into a blue rucksack. Finishing my coffee and toast I wiped the butter from my mouth and pulled the zip on the suitcase; it was like pushing a size twelve into a size ten pair of jeans.

It was mid August, two days before our wedding anniversary. The sun was rising and the sky was blue. We sat in our silver Ford Focus as I attached the Tom-tom to my windscreen and fed in the postcode for the cottage in The Mumbles, Swansea. Two hours later - having traversed the motorways and climbed the Heads of the Valley road - we were nearing Swansea. Holiday-makers trekked across the high street, making their way to the beach.

As we snaked up a farm track, the car wheels bumping over stones, the white cottage appeared, smoke swirling from a chimney amidst the thatched roof. "What a lovely place," my wife said, rubbing her hands with glee, "so near to the beach." Our footsteps crunched on the gravel walkway, the waves crashing against the rocks below. The cottage perched on a hillside, precariously overlooking the coastline.

Inserting the brass key into the dark brown door, it creaked as I pushed it open. As Megan looked around the lounge and kitchen I tugged the suitcase up the narrow wooden stairs. It was then that I noticed the locked door.

Since my childhood I loved mysteries. Sherlock Holmes was my hero. The first day of our holiday I was presented with a challenge: Could I open the lock without showing it had been disturbed? The chain gave a clank as I tested its strength.

"Leave it, Peter," Megan said loudly, "Maybe the owner has his own reasons for keeping it locked?"

"Yes I know. But I can hear a noise … something is in there," I said, appealing to my wife's curiosity, as she also placed her ear next to the door. By the third day I had decided that I should investigate further: so scaling the outside wall I climbed until my fingers reached the window ledge. Struggling to pull myself upwards I looked through the window and could see the inside of the locked room. Wiping dirt, sand and cobwebs from the glass I gazed as long as I could, before my arms weakened and I dropped to the ground below.

"There are some glass boxes. I think there could be animals in them," I stated to my partner in crime. "I think we should use a hacksaw and open the door: it could be a life of death situation if there are live animals." My wife nodded.

After a long period of sawing, the chain finally dropped to the cottage floor,with a clunk, as I pushed the door. Inside the room were snakes, lizards and other colourful reptiles moving inside glass and plastic containers. I felt my wife drawing back through the doorway, stumbling upon a metal ring on the floor. In the midst of the floor was a wooden hatch, which I struggled to lift, pulling hard on the metallic ring.

I carefully descended the spiralling stairs, which seemed to go on for ages, until - in my torchlight - I could see we were inside a large cave. The cold walls sent a shiver down my spine. I heard Megan gasp as she grabbed my arm: there was a middle-aged lady in a locked cage - she looked nervous until we explained we were holiday-makers.

Whspering hoarsley she said, "The man will be back soon. Quickly - the keys are on that table drawer." She pointed to an old wooden table.

Opening her prison we quickly looked for a way of escape. The sound of waves lapping became clearer. My wife tugged my sleeve, nervous that we could be stuck if we went further towards the sea.

We took the risk to ascend the stone stairs again: relieved that we were safe.

Back in the cottage I rang 999 on my mobile - and waited.

After what seemed like a lifetime a wave of blue lights shone through the windows. There was we heard a loud rapping on the door.

A voice called, "open up … it's the police!" Two burly men entered, complete with yellow fluorescent jackets.

The police told us that smugglers had operated from The Mumbles and the coast for centuries. The owner of the cottage was involved in an illegal trade in rare reptiles. Our holiday was cut short - but we had a tale to tell!

Chapter 8 Our Boy Wesley: A Poem

The doctor said, "We must take blood"
My lad complied, he was so good
Tests would follow
And Chemo too
We prayed so hard, "If only God would"

More tests came and surgery too
The boy took it all, whatever was due
Scans and needles
Days from home
We prayed again, joined a long queue

Wesley's mother stayed by his bed
Our son was brave, though tears were shed
Specialists visited
Nurses were kind
We prayed so long he wouldn't be dead

Months became four years of pain
He struggled on, taking the strain
Now in Heaven
Waiting for us

Some ask, "will we trust God again?"

Chapter 9 Congratulations: A Poem

Congratulations! Friends and family sang
Outside the church, bells' peel rang
Newly- wed couple walked the aisle
Groom and bride with beaming smile
Reception food plus speeches made
A honeymoon enjoyed, will joy fade?

The two now one with mortgage fee
Under pressure two become three
Love fades as things of beauty do
A reality check and baby's pooh
Time is cruel and passes fast
I question if the family will last

Others visit and bring support
Now friendship found that new love brought
So "they live happy ever after", and divorce thwart!

Chapter 10 An Author's Favourite Bible Verse

My favourite Bible Verse is Psalm 18:29:- "For by thee I have run through a troop; and by my God have I leaped over a wall."

I was made aware of this verse during the hardest time of my life. Our son, Wesley, had been diagnosed with cancer when he was three years old. As he entered hospital for tests and the start of his treatment I came across the verse. Whilst I did not have to face enemies after my life, as David, yet I was to pass through very trying days. Wesley endured weeks of chemotherapy, several times of surgery, and also radiotherapy. For four years, until he passed away, just after his seventh birthday, that verse helped me to find strength.

At Wesley's funeral I read the verse to the several hundred who attended, and there were few dry eyes. By God we can go through any difficulty, with His help we can get over seeming impossible obstacles. I have found in my struggles in church or family life, in business and my work, the promise of the verse lasts.

Chapter 11 A Man's Life Is Changed: A Poem

Jabez, the "misery-bringer"

Aspired to be a singer

But his life, once so stressed

Emerged as one Blessed

Zealously became "party-swinger"

Chapter 12 An Acrostic Encourager: Push

Pray

Until

Something

Happens

Chapter 13 The Phantom Flame-bringer

"Hell found me!" screamed John.

The flames licked around him as he raced down the school corridor. Knowing it was his doing made his predicament worse. Assuming his plan was flawless he dashed on breathlessly, panting and gasping for air. He was a firesetter, proud of his accomplishments until now.

Two weeks before Christmas I crawled out of bed.
Kissing my sleepy-eyed wife, "Sorry, hun, I have to go."
"Duh? Not again, Victor, this is no joke. Can't they call someone else?"

Getting quickly dressed I called, "See you soon" and left my warm house. By the time I reached the scene I knew we were chasing the flames again.

"Looks like him again, Mike," I intimated to the senior fire-fighter, as I nervously carried my video and stepladder towards the burning mass. "I need to get close to record the way this one grows."

"Yeah, I guess it is, Victor. Sure looks like his handy work. Don't get too close. This one will collapse the roof soon" the fireman warned me.

Black smoke billowed upwards, searing flames licking through broken windows, blue lights spinning around casting eerie shadows across the playground. Gigantic snake-like hoses pulsed and gyrated with high pressure jets of water. Sights I will never forget. In my seven years as a Fire Investigation officer I had never seen such speedy devastation. I knew then my evidence had to be meticulous, detailed and thorough.

"I need to get closer, Mike, so I can get a good recording"

"Okay, Victor, I will get the lads to spray some jets over you."

The cool spray splattered all around me. I felt the pressure of the water jets pushing me forwards. It was important to record the inferno as it took hold. My job was to examine, record and present conclusions to the school, police, insurance and Fire Service. The Blue Coat School was not the first. Readers of my report would associate it with me; it was inevitable, headed and signed Victor McDonald. Standing on the metal steps as close as I dare, I stretched my 5ft. 6" frame to record with the JVC VCR.

My eyebrows were singed, perspiration dripped from my forehead as I leaned against the top of the ladder recording as speedily as I could. I disliked the white safety helmet but was glad it offered some protection, my grey-haired ponytail tucked up inside. The heat erupted like Mt. Vesuvius belching blazing sparks and glass shards over my head like fireworks.

"This is getting out of control, sir, you had better get back," one of the uniformed fire-fighters shouted to me.

"Okay, I am through I think, until I can enter the building."

The December night sky was lit up like Bonfire Night. Choking clouds spiraled towards the moon, causing it to hide its face. Smoldering embers smoked around the engines as dark-uniformed fire-fighters bedecked in yellow overalls streamed more water towards the sweltering fury. Pieces of debris was spitting, sparkling, sizzling and hissing hitting the sides of the building and the playground. I ducked, sliding quickly down the stepladder. It would be some hours before I could enter the blackened and charred remains.

The time was one fifteen in the morning on December 11 Arson is the purposeful lighting of fires that cause damage to the environment, property and people.

Fortunately, nobody was injured on that occasion. I prepared my report on the West Midlands serial arsonist. Based on the number of events, their frequency and locations, arson is classified by type as single, double, triple, mass, spree or serial. We were dealing with a vendetta-led person, getting bolder and more dangerous every blaze. In England in an average week our communities suffer over 1200 serious fires, 50 injuries, 2 deaths and cost to society of £45 million, instigated by Firesetters.

Such was the impact to Local Authority buildings that serious resources had been made available. A dedicated team of experienced professional had been released from their day jobs to give solid focus to finding the culprit. It was none o' clock in the morning the day after the Blue Coat School fire when the team came together. In a room next to the Deputy Fire Chief's office I faced my six colleagues, a mix of 3 fire-fighters one CID sergeant, an Insurance loss-adjuster and a criminal profiler.

"Okay, listen up, people," I gathered everyone's attention. "It looks like Porky has struck again. Let's focus and brainstorm on what we know, see if we're missing anything."

Mark, the Profiler, gave us his heads up.

"He's a male, early to late teens, low achiever at school, probably unemployed. "

"That fits half the teenage population," one of my team suggested.

"His habitation is within a radius of five miles of the targeted area," the profiler continued.

"Makes sense, we know he gets to the scene on a pushbike, according to a witness," my second-in-command added.

"Problems with long-term relationships could well have been abused as a child or bullied, in a dysfunctional family. Motives could vary: - an excitement and adrenalin rush; curiosity and fascination with fire; anti-social and destructive behaviour; an expressive cry for help, a compulsion that was uncontrollable."

"And he's a fat bastard," Sean, one of the senior Fire and Rescue Officers commented. "We know that from a witness at one of the earlier scenes."

"Thanks, everyone," I nodded to the team, "anyone else got something?

On the glass screen-wall facing us were photos of the fires, press releases, significant findings at the scene. We knew that few arson investigations resulted in criminal prosecution. Our combined knowledge and experience would be pooled to spotlight the locations of the LEA buildings set on fire in the previous twenty-four months, types of fire, circumstances that were special. Every fire has a signature of its own. The team were reading signs and listening to the whispers, chasing the flames.

....

John Stokes combed his black hair, making a parting down the middle. Placing his metal-wired rounded spectacles over his bulbous nose he examined his pot-marked skin for new blemishes. Struggling to pull his size 16 black tee-shirt over his size 22 girth he shouted to his mother.

"Mother you have shrunk my favourite tee-shirt. You can't do anything right, you old bat!" Refusing to take the bait, Beryl Stokes called up the stairs. "There's a red one in your drawer." "BLACK, you know I love black," John exclaimed. His day was ruined because his idiot mother couldn't use a washing machine properly. He did not consider that he had put on weight. Since twelve stone at twelve years old he had ballooned to eighteen stone by his seventeenth birthday in the summer.

"I'm going to the allotment," he announced slamming the front door.

Beryl was secretly glad that her troubled boy had left the house. It gave her some private time with Daytime TV. Since her husband had passed away, occupied her moments dreaming of better days and fending off her son's abuse.

Still seething over his confrontation at home John, or Porky, as the fire investigation team had named him, kicked the shed door shut and surveyed his possessions in his workshop lair. Most of the items in the allotment shed belonged to his late father. New acquisitions were instant camera, cork-board, petrol cans and empty coke bottles. Attached to the board were four Polaroid snaps of burnt buildings, taken the day after each fire.

As he pinned a new photo to his treasured snaps John welled with pride, "Yes, the phantom flame-bringer strikes again!"

Contrary to what the population felt about him John didn't regard himself as a monster. He was a craftsman, a master at his art. His blackened graffiti was testimony to his prowess. Life was never in danger, in his opinion, he was "sticking it to the bastards who had given him grief", getting his own back from teachers who failed him.

Fire had held a fascination for John since his junior school days. Lighting fires in the woods at the back of Dudley Zoo he had been mesmerized by the tongues of heat. He could put up with the smell of smoke on his clothes if he had experienced a good blaze. By his teens the ability to consume, devour, melt, roast and char gave him an instrument of power. Fires became his weapons of choice. Fire-play became malicious fire-setting which evolved into pyromania. His West Midlands crusade had started two years before Blue Coat School burned to the ground. Each gap between the fires was getting shorter. The next one was being planned in his disturbed head.

"This one will be ace!" he proclaimed aloud, knowing that he was the sole audience.

I was having rare moments at home before gathering the team together again. My first marriage had suffered due to my commitment to the Fire and Rescue Service. Sally, and I don't blame her, never knew when or if I would be home. In the end our strained relationship ended. Two years ago I proposed to Becky and happily she said "yes". My job with Investigations was nowhere near as dangerous, but the hours were just as demanding. Especially if we were faced with the challenges we had with Porky.

"I am sorry about the other night, Becks. It was a school. We need to catch this bastard."

"It's alright, Victor, just sometimes I wish we had more times like this," Becky wistfully gazed at me.

Relishing pepperoni pizza and a visit to the salad bar at Pizza Hut, Becky and I were enjoying a romantic interlude from our busy work schedules. Having our second top-up of coffee we held hands across the table, unembarrassed to show affection. My mobile bleeped a text message.

"No, it cannot be!" I exclaimed staring at the message. "Sorry, Becky, I must go, the fire is next to a residential area."

Becky's knuckles were white as she held them tightly in a ball, "Well if you must."

The phantom flame-bringer saw the blue flashing lights appearing over the horizon. Unsatisfied with the fire's slow progress, he walked along the corridor to the gym, sprinkling petrol as he walked. Thinking, mistakenly, he was walking away from the flames, towards the hall entrance, John threw a lighted match over his shoulder and smirked.

"That should do it," he announced with glee, "I will take a photo at the back of the school, where I left my bike." John often talked to himself, maybe because no-one else would listen to his rants.

His colossal mistake had been to underestimate the flammability of the old ceiling tiles. All of his previous conquests had been modern schools, many having
Acoustic tiles and sprinkler systems, which John disengaged as he worked. On this fatal occasion the master-planner had failed to properly survey the buildings.

"Oh shit! John shouted as he entered the gym. By opening the door he caused an updraft that rose towards him. The flames were chasing oxygen and he stood in their way.

"Run, you fat bugger, back up the corridor!"

Alas, it was too late for John Stokes. Hell found him and so did I; amongst the blackened devastation were the charred remains of a human body. Dental records established his identity. Police gave the sad news to his mother.

"He's a good boy," Beryl sobbed. "It's since he lost his father he went to pieces."

Later the SOCO team removed evidence from the allotment shed.

The phantom flame-bringer, AKA "Porky" would set no more fires.

Chapter 14 A Trip Of A Lifetime: The Comper's Reward

I remember the day. A letter came from "Cacharel Pour L'homme" in an embossed yellow envelope. Rushing into the kitchen I announced my win.

"I have won an all expenses adventure holiday to the USA"
"That's wonderful, who will you take?" my funny wife quipped.
"Look at this! We are to attend the prize-giving presentation at The Kensington Palace Hotel in London"
"I will need a new dress", she winked her eye hopefully.

I had been doing consumer competitions for a few years, and subscribed to Competitors Companion, which gave advance details of prizes. Cacharel was a well-known perfume and after-shave giant. The challenge of entering competitions was getting the products and leaflets. With that prize I also smelled better for months.

The competition centred on "The Six-million dollar man", with questions and slogan to compete. My slogan was "The Cacharel man knows where he's going, others scents where he's been." Alongside five other couples we were off to the adventure of a lifetime.

The presentation itself was enough to satisfy any comper. We were wined and dined in Kensington at a really posh place. In our room was every product that Cacharel made: shower gels, perfume, talc, after-shave, bath salts etc. We were spoiled rotten!

The downside to the award was the scary video about white-water rafting, rapids, snakes, heat that would fry you. My wife was more nervous about the holiday after the show. Looking back I am amazed that she joined in as she doesnt like snakes or danger. Does anybody?

June soon came along. We were flying to Grand Junction in Colorado. The Ramada Inn was our first taste of real luxury. As everything was paid by the company, I had steak, steak and more steak! After a swim and relaxing night in the hotel we were a bit nervous about the trip the next day.

The guides collected the party of 12 in two jeeps. We were off to the river. I don't have a fear of water, so was looking forward to shooting the Colorado rapids. Entering the swirling waters in baking heat we boarded three black rubber dinghies. During the lull, when we drifted with the current, I jumped into the waters.

Feeling a bump against my leg I asked the guide what that could be. "The catfish here can be four feet". I just hoped they were vegetarian fish.

We were assured that there were no dangerous water snakes. Our guide sought to encourage us, but failed: "Rattlers are a different thing. Just back away."

The first night we slept in two-man tents by the side of a noisy churning river. Inky blackness was broken by foaming swirls. Well at least I slept in the tent; my wife was too hot so slept outside.The sound of crashing water kept us awake. Toliet was a metal can fifty feet from the site. My adventure partner was not impressed with that either!

We enjoyed a bar-b-cue at the campsite. It was the first time I had lobster. Think it may be my last.

On the next day we shot "The Skull rapids" in Westwater Canyon. I was relieved when that was over. If you got stuck there they, had to helicopter you out in a harness. No wonder we had filled in a Disclaimer!

Our guide was smoking grass. Not the best model of survival for us newbies. We splashed and sploshed to his instructions: "Thump that tube". I even paddled.
The military use the rapids for training, surging through the water in life-jackets.

Finally we reached the "exit or pull-out point". Vehicles took us to Moab in Utah. More steak! We had a short quiz that evening. I was the only one who knew about Ruth in the Bible and Moab. Much of Utah was inhabited by Mormons, who gave Bible names to places. Years later my family and I visited Salt Lake City and were impressed by the grandeur.

For the end section of our adventure we flew over The Grand Canyon. The wife loved it, I felt sick. The air currents ride you up and down like a fair-ground ride. The passenger door in the four-seater Cessna was flapping, I thought dangerously. The canyon was a huge chasm of rock ,the river resembling a tiny cotton thread hundreds of feet below. Once again our guide attempted to encourage us: "It's only dangerous if you drop below others Line of Sight. A chopper bought it last month." God, where do they train these guides I thought?

We spent two amazing days and nights in Las Vegas. The Hilton Hotel was luxurious. Sadly it is no longer there. In the casinos I was perplexed to observe that most people playing the slot machines were poor Hispanic women. They were hoping for a jackpot. At the card, dice and roulette tables there were ordinary folk and a few "high-rollers". Because all the accommodation, meals and travel was paid for I chanced my arm and lost £5.

Tom Jones was not performing the nights we stayed in Vegas, which gutted my Mrs. The best show was a famous magician who made the Eiffel Tower disappear on TV. It cost about £75 to see him, so my money stayed secure in my pocket.

The final part of our amazing holiday was four nights in San Francisco. Taken from the airport in a sleek black Limousine I could see the city skyline. I could easily live in San Francisco. There is just the right balance between old and new. I thought of detectives Cagney and Lacey as we rode the Trolley car up and down the hills. China town was incredible.

Opting to visit Al Catraz, I was glad that I did. It was almost a decaying monument, but the condemned cells were working. I spent a few minutes that seemed like hours in the isolated darkness. When the metal rods go "CLANG" you know you are locked in. The ranger let me out, much to my loved ones relief. She was about to petition the Governor.

Meals at night were mainly at Madame Wong's. Overlooking San Soledo and The Golden Gate Bridge it is an incredible location. The course kept coming. New bowls with exotic substances were placed in the centre of the revolving circular table. I dished what I wanted and spun the table. There must have been over forty servings. I met Madame Wong, not sure if she was the original as she looked quite young.

Back home I continued to enter competions. We went to Amsterdam courtesy of Mars Bars, I won £100 in vouchers which the kids had for music CD's. My near miss was a Villa on the Costa Del Sol. My caption, for Amber Solaire, was "One good tan deserves another".

I think it should have won. What about you?

Chapter 15 Let Go Then What? : A Poem Of Faith's Struggles

"Let go and trust" the voice above said
If I obeyed I may be dead
Faith is fine with safety net
If not I rocket like a flechette
Shooting downwards with my head

A surgeon's scalpel I have to trust
My wife's love and cooking if I must
But to accept someone I cannot see
Is pretty hard, at least to me.
If faith's not used it tends to rust

I flex faith's muscles when I can
Strong or weak, just like a man
No use pretending put on a face
In for the long-haul, not a race
No religion claims me as a fan

Chapter 16 Home Wreckers

They came in the night and wrecked my home.

My family was scattered, fleeing to safe havens. I sat alone in the inky darkness. Who would do such a thing and why?

It could have been the wind. Had blowing blustery breezy breaths caused my structure to topple? Or was it enemies I had made - jealous of my designs? Elaborate constructions well known ... the envy of many.

No. This was not a chance gust of air. It was not the demented wrath of a rival. This devastation spoke of THEM! Predators who swoop like winged phantoms. Whispers in our family lore spoke of Giant Troll-like home-wreckers - who have no regard for property or edifice ... All they know is pull down and destroy.

Slithering like slimy snakes in the shadowy starlit night, they wrecked my habitat. Ripping, tearing it apart, and throwing it down to the ground piece by piece. Nothing was left but a vacuous hole, tormenting me for not building stronger.

"Next time I will make it stronger," I reasoned. Why procrastinate? I spun a new line and dropped. Attaching the peripheral anchors I began, to weave my web. It would be bigger, better and bastion-like this time! Let them come!

Chapter 17 A Boy Is Trapped

"Please help! Read this note. You can find me and help me. I want to get home. I know it must be bad to use the mirrors. Please. I promise I won't do it again."

My name is Stephen Brown. The first time I did it was at my grandma's. I loved working in her gardens. It was fun to sell stuff on market days. The coolest thing was having a bedroom of my own. Sharing a bedroom at home with my two brothers was a pain in the bum.

My room had a bed, dresser and wardrobe. I don't know what made me do it, but one day I was looking in the dresser mirror and reached out to touch it. Imagine my surprise when my arm travelled through. I am not stupid, I know that should not happen, and I am not lying.

Soon I followed with my whole body! I entered a room with lots of doors with name plates on: - Ship; Wood: Market: Garden; Castle… I decided to try one or two.

Most of the places have been pretty good. I have only seen people, though, at the market and castle. But the people in the castle will not let me get back to the mirror in the armoury, so I can't get home. I have put this note in my lunch-box and thrown it out the window. Please do what you can and get me home!

Chapter 18 Braveheart: An Acrostic Poem

Bravely he walks into the fray
Remembering others who walked away
A cost so high not willing to pay
Victory comes at high price today

Eternity beckons not faraway
Hearts will mourn the costs outweigh
Enduring pain and feel castaway
A soldier's lot is straightaway

Rescuing those who breakaway
To believe lives are not thrown away.

Chapter 19 Frozen Fish: How Not To Cook

I remember the day. It was a day when my manly pride suffered a blow from a six year old.

"There's ice in my fish."

That was not what I wanted to hear from my daughter.

Examining the offending meal I had to admit it did look like ice on the cod. Sampling mine, I admitted defeat.

"Sorry, Rachel, I had better read the instructions again."

What I failed to observe on Birds Eye Cod in Buttered Sauce was that the thirty minutes cooking in boiling water assumed the fish was defrosted. It was a family trait to leap without looking, to press ahead blindly paying no regard to instructions. Not a good plan if you are parachuting or serving meals to a six year old gastronome.

Okay, so I am not the best cook in the world. Probably not the best cook in our street. On that day it appeared I was not even qualified to compare to a six-year olds' ability to provide a meal. On a scale of 1 to 10 I think I got a 1.

My wife, Margaret, was in London at GOSH caring for our middle child. Cooking, cleaning, doing the washing were my responsibilities. My good turn had gone badly wrong. Initially, I was planning to take my daughter and two year old son to McDonalds or Pizza Hut, but I was persuaded by some cookery programme that I could cope. Some hope! I was deflated like a punctured tyre.

Good turns are fine if you have read the rule-book or recipe. Next time I did instant mash potatoes with fish, I ensured the meal was cooked.

"Dad, I think you have burnt it!".

Bah!

Chapter 20 Memories At A Funeral: Life & Death

Gordon died. The vicar said he had gone to his place of rest.

A Native American believes in a "happy hunting ground", taking bows and arrows, riding his pony across eternal plains, no white settler to steal his land.

Norsemen or Vikings have their Valhalla. Sword in their right hand they would hold it high and shout "ODIN!" The body placed on board a sailing boat and set adrift, flaming arrows would reach their target and the Viking chieftain would be cremated at sea, his soul to live on raping and pillaging.

Egyptian pharaohs would be rolled in tight perfumed strips of white cloth. Mummified they were placed in ornate coffins and secured in crypts hundreds of feet beneath the sand. Their favorite wives and servants would be killed to join them. Pharaohs did not relish the idea of waking up in their after life alone.

Memories are strange things. Family events such as funerals bring a kaleidoscope of images from our past, playing them as a cinema reel onto our conscious mind. At my brother-in-law's funeral while the vicar read passages from the Bible my mind was elsewhere. I reflected on grandma and granddad, mum and dad, aunt and uncle, friends from school and work and above all our son Wesley. I wondered where they were. Could they look down upon us watching us, participating in our lives? Had we said our goodbyes and adieus like the Vera Lynn song, "We'll meet again, don't know how, and don't know when."?

Would Gordon wake up somewhere alone as we recalled his life? Was he watching us as we sang "The Lord's My Shepherd"?

His idea of Heaven would be a night at the Ebbw Vale Labour Club with Michael Foot the main speaker and free beer. He was an adamant and loudly verbal supporter of the Labour Party, proud to be named after Nye Bevan. Stones dedicated to Aneurin Bevan were placed in the grassland at the peek of The Heads of The Valley Road.

Ebbw Vale and the Welsh valleys were proud of the originator of the National Health Service and as Bill said a few weeks before he died in 2012, "Nye would turn in his grave if he knew what the Tories were doing to the NHS!" If they allowed flags in Gordon's heaven he would be flying the Red One.

I was not sure what I believed about "life after death". Enduring the vicar at Gordon's funeral drone on and on caused me to plan my own arrangements which would be lodged with our solicitor, with my Will. My funeral plan would be simple:-

As my coffin was brought into the crematorium, not a church, the mourners would hear "Always look on the bright side of life" played over the speakers. The cortege would be accompanied by clowns and jugglers. There would be no sermon, just a reading from the Gospel of john chapter 14. I was hedging my bets about a mansion waiting for me. As the part was being read about "ashes to ashes" and my coffin descended to the abyss, a Scots piper would play "The Last Post". Frank Sinatra's rendition of "My Way" would play as the congregation left the auditorium to celebrate my life with a buffet meal and a pint at the pub. Job done.

Our memories of childhood may not be real memories. I don't mean that the events were not real. The recall of them is not ours; we have been told our life journey by another, as tribal elders gather youngsters in their tepee or hut, sharing the lore of the community.

My first "real" memory, one that I owned, was my being at a party with Union Jack banners. We ate sandwiches and trifle. Trifles were for Christmas so I knew that day was special. A Coronation Mug was in my hands as we walked home along the canal. I was three. Queen Elizabeth II was inaugurated on that day.

At that time we lived in Canal Street, Congleton. Our bath was a tin one. Bath-time was kept warm by the heat from the coal hearth fire. The toilet was outside, a short walk up the yard. Cuts from newspaper were on a nail behind the door, just in case the toilet paper ran out.

The second memory was of my brother Michael, two years older than me, biting the doctor's leg. He was a sickly child up to his early teens. When the GP called Mike crept from his lair under the table and chewed on the physician's leg.

My third and probably fondest memory from my days as a toddler was splashing about in the River Dane at Somerford, near to my grandparents' farm. A family photo shows me nude; fortunately the river water was up to my waist and muddy. My two brothers were making a damn across the swirling river. I was looking at the camera, a white body, white face and red hair.

Other photos in our family album were taken at the farm. One showed me sitting in a wicker skip peering out. Too high for a toddler to climb our mum would place me in there to be certain where I would be. In the photo her arm was clearly visible at the edge. She rarely looked good in a photo. In nearly all the pictures of mum with dad she is standing on one leg like a stork, even their wedding photo.

My uncle Sid, my mother's brother-in-law, was the first relative to die that I could recall. A navy man he had large anchor tattoos on his forearms. We didn't have a TV at that time. Mum and I used to go to his and Aunty Mabel's bungalow to view "Watch with Mother". I still remember "Rag Tag and Bobtail", "Andy Pandy" and "Bill and Ben the Flowerpot Men". He died on a bus.

Granddad Joe, my mum's dad, died while I was in my first year at Grammar School. My mother's mum died when mum was 12 so I never knew her. Joe lived with us. On Saturdays I would polish his hob-nailed boots for half a crown. Those boots, with metal studs, were to be my downfall quite literally. In our house at Sefton Avenue near the station I skated on the quarry tile hallway in Joe's clogs, slipped and broke my arm. The fracture resulted in my first visit to A & E at the War Memorial Hospital.

At Christmas he would give me a ten shilling note. That was a lot to me. You could buy bagfuls of sherbet fizzes with ten shillings.

I wasn't party to his funeral. I have no idea how mum or her sister felt. His goal for an after-life I supposed would to be working in the coalmine at Whitfield Colliery, where he was a foreman, and coming home to his wife and young daughters.

My father's dad, Fred. Passed away suddenly, or so I thought. He always seemed so strong. He taught me so much about farming and life in general. Fred took everything in his stride.

Every school holiday I was dropped off to stay at the farm. The farm was a safe place to keep me for a few weeks. It was safe until I stuck a gardening fork through my welly, through my foot and into the soil. Fred examined my toes and foot, wiped them with dettol and said I would live. I didn't go to hospital on that occasion.

Feeding the hens was simple. Tip the corn from the feed bin into a bucket, carry it into the chicken run and pour it into the feeding troughs. Sometimes toast and bacon rind leftovers were added. I filled the hens drinking troughs with water using a hosepipe, tempted repeatedly to place my finger at the nozzle and shower the birds. I only did that once. Fred had a big hand.

My granddad had a gun. It was a double-barrel shotgun which leaned by the main door in their passageway. Dad's sister "rode with the hounds" to chase down foxes. My grand-parents and my dad regarding the four-legged predators as vermin. Shooting them was kinder than "The Hunt".

When I was 12, under supervision, I pulled down the barrel, inserted two 1210 cartridges into the chambers and went with dad and granddad into the fields. The farm was more of a market garden than farm. The fields were rented to larger farms for their crops and there was no livestock except the chickens. It was to protect the feathered "livestock" that we three carefully strode through wheat fields looking for "sign". Firing at the fleeing red animals with bushy tails, I have never shot another weapon. The hole made in the little fox's side horrified me. Innards, ribs, gore, coagulated blood and mangled fur was on the ground. It was breathing its last when we arrived. From then on I left shooting to sideshows at the fairground or aiming at tin-cans with my 2.2 air rifle.

Fred's funeral service left no memory apart from food and drink. I was in my late teens and the refreshments were at The Black Swan at Arclid. Dad called the pub "The Mucky Duck".

My grandfather's death brought huge changes. It happened so quickly after my grand-parents moving into our street. Dad continued to work as a Patrolman in the AA. One of my fondest memories as a child was hearing his Automobile Association motorbike pull up. Dad would park and come up the passageway whistling. Whistling must have been a family trait. Over years the motorbike was replaced by an Austin mini-van. When Senior Patrol William Alfred Worthington retired he was driving a Rangerover.

My grandma, Nellie died at 84; next dad died at 76, and finally mums death came at 84.

I read brief notes at both of my parents' funerals. Mum was born in May 1921, dad in July. She said he was her "toy-boy". "Alf" as he liked to be known fought in the Second World War. He was in the desert against Rommel and ended up landing at the Sicily landing against the Italians.

The effects of war lasted for years. My dad told me once that he had seen men running through barbed-wire so fast they left strips of cloth and skin behind. I suppose many soldiers had witnessed horror.

Other funerals I had attended, school friends, brought to my mind snap images of school life. One term a friend did not come back to school. He had drowned in the summer trying to swim the canal and got caught in weeds. It was a sad time. Grief was short-lived as I didn't know his family.

The vicar was finally doing the bit about "dust to dust".

Prior to arriving at the Crematorium the cortege had travelled along the main roads until it arrived at Ebbw Vale. Slowing down the funeral hearse was saluted by waiting crowds in the streets. A few white roses landed on the top of the coffin-bearing vehicle. In the South Wales tradition streets were lined with mourners two deep.

Twenty minutes after leaving Ebbw Vale the cortege arrived at the Crematorium, off the Swansea Dual carriageway. "Men of Harlech" played over the speakers, a very moving rendition by the Tredegar Male Voce Choir. We had heard them several times at Brierley Hill Town hall.

The meal was held at a local pub. Accommodating thirty officially there were about fifty people, locals popped in and out. In huddles around the room people balanced paper plates containing a variety of buffet food and shared stories of Gordon,

Amidst the memories of loss there is always the smiling image of a little boy. John Wesley Worthington, born Jan 4th 1977, died in January 1984. There are real memories of Great Ormond Street Hospital, surgery, radiotherapy and chemo. My mind has memories of hair loss, needles, vomiting, tears, constant journeys from Suffolk to London, images of a small boy who was dying. Childhood cancer called "Neuroblastoma" had lurked in my boy's body, to usher in a world of doctors and nurses, other parents, medical equipment that bleeped. A maelstrom of anguish opened on our wedding anniversary when we were first informed of Wesley's cancer.

When Wesley's funeral cars made there way to Ipswich cemetery it had snowed heavily. His uncles left their vehicles to push the hearse up a hill, Gordon was there. Maybe he has joined my boy in another world and they laugh about that.

Chapter 21 Battle For The Planets: A Game

BATTLE FOR THE PLANETS: The Purple Planet

My phone alarm woke me at six thirty - September 1st had finally arrived - I leapt out of bed with an adrenalin rush. Shaving and showering quickly, I hurriedly pulled on my Lee jeans and tee-shirt, hopping to the front door as I inserted my feet into trainers.

"Bye, Mum", I called, "See ya in a while," closing the door, crunching on the gravel path I opened my car door. "Please start", I thought, as I turned the ignition. The Ford Focus roared into action as I sped down the dual carriageway towards the Shopping Centre. Parking next to the Odeon cinema I made my way through the glass doors, which opened automatically with a "swish". The Merry Hill Centre was open from seven. Buying a paper I sat in McDonalds eating the Early Breakfast, keeping my eye on my watch and the shop opposite.

GAME, its purple neon letters unlit, was immersed in darkness, but already a queue was forming. The retail chain had agreed to open early, at eight, sensing there would be demand for the latest expansion pack from BlizzCom. Cutting into my last remnants of sausage and hash brown, I looked again through the restaurant windows as I scanned the twenty or so faces outside GAME - Unsurprised that I didn't recognise anyone. My black coffee smelt good as I raised the Styrofoam cup; the bitterness challenging my taste buds to wake up.

At seven forty I stood with other online gamers, electric tingles in my spine, as I thought of the next week. I booked the days as my annual leave months before, knowing I would need the time to learn new skills; find routes; acquire equipment and meet personnel: and especially build and explore the new star system - The Purple Planet.

Since BlizzCom had launched "Battle of the Planets" five years ago it had grown in popularity to be a major online success. Three expansions packs later: "The Purple Planet" being the fourth - there were fifteen million players worldwide, all paying a monthly subscription of eight pounds ninety-nine pence a month. My character "Petros" had been "ghosted" at level eighty for months, my hands grew clammy as I thought of the details of the Expansion and what it offered.

In Computer Weekly and Forums I had read with a thrill that "The Purple Planet" offered players: leveling to eight-five, Light-speed from our Milky Way to Alpha Centauri and the Cygnus Constellation to the Purple Planet and its moon, an additional space for a sixth crew member, better weapons and transport, plus the usual extra levels for professions like Mining and First Aid. Customers who bought the "Special" version would also have the benefit of giving crew members names and enhancements to their ship.

The purple GAME sign spluttered casting an eerie glow as the shutters were raised with a metallic grating sound, and finally the shop door opened. After minutes that seemed like a lifetime, I was at the counter.

"Hi", I said to the assistant, who shook his head to flick a straying black hair strand backwards, "I've ordered The Purple Planet , the name is Bailey: Marcus Bailey."

Opening an A4 binder, tracking columns with his finger, the assistant said, "The Special Edition? That'll be fifty nine pounds and ninety nine pence." I heard somebody behind me say, "Lucky sod".

Inserting my Halifax bank card into the machine, I pressed the buttons and enter. The assistant placed the precious parcel into a GAME bag, handing it across the counter, as the next customer approached. Checking the box as I walked quickly toward the centre exit, I read some of the main features; my stomach churning. Placing my cargo carefully on the passenger seat, deciding a seat-belt wouldn't fit around it; I fired up the car and left the car park for home.

"That you?" Marcus, a voice called from the kitchen.

"Yes, Mum, it's me. *"If it was the mad-axe man you'd be dead by now,"* I spoke silently as I took the stairs two at a time.

"Want some breakfast?" Mum called after me.

"No thanks, I ate in the mall, I'm gonna be busy all day, so don't worry about lunch n' stuff."

"Playing that bloody game, I bet", a rough voice bellowed from the kitchen, "fancy having a week off to play games: he's got more money than sense."

"Hush, Jim, it could be a lot worse - he could be out-of-work, on drugs or out every night." I heard mum say.

The hairs on the back of my neck were standing up as I ripped open the cardboard box, inserting the CD into my computer drive. After a few moments of whirring, my screen changed to a video introducing "The Purple Planet", as the scroll bar moved slowly from no percent towards one hundred. Picking up a can of Red Bull I popped it open, slurping the cool drink, as I read again the features of the expansion pack as my PC worked away, my mind struggling to remember what I'd read over the past months.

The installation menu said, "Complete", and immediately my screen changed to my standard log-in menu. My fingers seemed to have a mind of their own as I typed player code and password - the familiar image of my character appeared - Commander Petros, Lieutenant Colonel of Star Command - I clicked "Enter" and waited ... and waited...

Looking at the new menu I tested the icons. "My experience bar is no longer frozen at eighty, I could start to level again," I thought ... "Now what else is new?"

A voice caught my attention in my headset, "Good morning, Marcus, how's your day?" It was Commander Dorke, or real name Stefan, a student in Sweden. "... Have you checked anything out yet?"

"Na," I replied, "... only just got home ...you?"

"I'm on my home planet, visiting trainers and suppliers - gonna collect some quests in a sec," the voice sounded loud in my ear-piece. My online friends and I used Skype rather than the online audio-speak, finding it better quality and it didn't interfere with in-game messages.

"I left my ship over Earth last night, making it my home-port - so I am gonna hearth-stone and look around NYC," I said. "I know there are two quests at The Senate and White House. Do you know where the ambassador quest-line starts?" I asked, taking another swig of Red Bull.

"Being an ice-man from Uranus I am not sure, Earthling; have you checked the inn for Speech bubbles?" Stefan suggested, with a hint of his sarcastic humour.

"Yeah, yeah. OK, Commander Dorke.... I'll speak to ya later."

Apart from some changes to the Graphical Interface, I knew my Special Edition had some extra exclusive features: one was naming my crew. Clicking on "Crew Menu", I brought up my Military Expert - a huge green Orc appeared, armed to the teeth, "good day, Commander Petros, what can I do for you?" Using Edit I re-named him "Arnie", wishing I could give him an Austrian accent. Smiling I said, "I'll be back", and my character walked from the inn in New York City, to hail a cab.

I became my character as role-playing kicked in. Like all players around the world, I made no distinction between Marcus Bailey, IT support worker, and Commander Petros. It was me flying a Star-ship, giving commands, exploring galaxies and killing the bad guys.

My flight ability on Earth was "unavailable", so I couldn't use my ship's shuttle. I determined I must pay that fine before I leave Earth: I also needed to visit the Bank.

Earth, being a democracy, unlike many planets or systems, had a Senate and President. I headed for The Boulevard, with Arnie following, his huge eight-foot tall and three hundred pounds squeezed into the yellow and white taxi, as it speeded on the NYC grid system, tires squealing round corners, until we arrived with a jolt.

Ascending the marble stairway we faced a number of doors, all with metallic nameplates. Clicking on "Training" I entered the oblong room, looking for any trainers I didn't recognize - there were none. Visiting each in turn I gathered documents on: Navigational Flight Paths; Language & Factions; Medicals and First Aid; Communications, Engineering and Ship enhancements; Military and Arms. Visiting my Profession Trainers - I was a Miner and a Skinner- I took certificates from them. Dragging documents out of my bag, I placed them in the bags of my crew members, once skills were learned the documents disappeared.

The next door Arnie and I went through was "Senate". Making our way through the chamber there was a yellow exclamation mark over the Senate Leader, the overweight balding figure seated in an ornate chair, like a throne. Taking the quests to "explore and colonize The Purple Planet", and "Visit the President" I said, "Thank you, Sir"; I sent co-ordinates and flight path to my Flight Control. Clicking on the figure next to him: looking like a judge; I paid my fine, noticing the Earth flight ban lifted.

Visiting The President of Earth, who resembled Abraham Lincoln, I received a "For Your Eyes Only" quest - My mission to rescue an Earthling who was stranded on the massive Purple Planet moon.

Using my hearthstone, I transported back to the Inn -The Coyote Ugly- , allocating two thousand dollars to each crew member, and placing them on "automatic", so they could gather supplies. Walking to The Bank I transferred a hundred thousand dollars to the ship's account, changing half to "Zlots" - the interplanetary currency. Commander Petros and his crew were ready…

"Have you found that other quest yet?" Stefan spoke into my headset.
"Bugger. I'm glad you reminded me, I was just about to teleport to The Falcon and leave", I said, annoyed at myself.
and leave", I said, annoyed at myself.

"Look for a guy with a beard -a bit like Gandalf- he is sitting in the kitchen area of the Inn … it's an escort quest … pays well," Stefan added. "Listen, I'm supposed to be revising, but when you start building on the Purple Planet, buzz me online, and we can help each other … huh?"

"Great idea mate", I replied. "Before you go, do you know when Carol is coming online?"

"I think she is on nights, so may be on later," he hung up Skype.

Carole, or Princess Leila, Commander, was a Venusian in-game, and a red-headed nurse in real-life, who lived in Sheffield as a single mum. We met at the launch of the expansion pack at The Metropole Hotel in Birmingham.

Descending the wooden stairs to the Inn's kitchen, a speech bubble was over the head of a character at the table. Ambassador Grey needed to be transported to the Cygnus Constellation and escorted to his embassy - the fee was two hundred thousand zlots. Accepting the quest, he became part of my crew, occupying the new sixth slot.

Teleporting to The Falcon, there was a buzz and excitement on the Flight Deck, coloured lights flashed at modules, several screens opened before my eyes. Pressing the "auto-pilot" button and pushing the lever to "Hyper-drive", white lights whizzed by, like speeding through a tunnel.

Coming out of hyper-space to my mind was like jumping off an escalator, the crew and I lurched forwards as a purple orb appeared, overshadowed by a huge white cratered moon, other moons appearing in the distance. Arnie and I boarded the two-man shuttle and jetted to the planet's surface. Using my hand-held Comms I called the Engineer Expert, who one day I would re-name "Scotty"…

"Good day, Commander Petros …what can I do for you?" I clicked "return shuttle to ship"

A few moments later the Engineer Expert's icon was flashing red, I gave the command for the Building Expert and a Builder to board the shuttle and join us on the planet.

The shuttle appeared out of the haze around the planet, and I set the workers to build living quarters, communications and teleport centre, power plant and then on "auto-build". As the building workers toiled away, walls appearing, sounds of sawing and hammering, Arnie and I flew from the compound, then disembarked to explore. Walking into an inky-blackness, the terrain appeared as it was "discovered", and a map of the area grew. Blue lights flashed, indicating mining nodules, so I set Arnie on "Auto-explore" as I mined with my pick-axe. Silver, Iron and Obsidium ores began to fill my bags.

Arnie's face icon started to glow red, his health dropping from a hundred percent to ninety to eighty. Jumping aboard the shuttle, I carefully maneuvered the craft to follow Arnie's trail. The last thing I needed was to prang the machine in a tree. Carcasses appeared on the desert ground beneath me as I reached the edge of the explored territory, Arnie was below me striking a gigantic worm with his broad-sword. Hurrying towards him I applied a medical dressing as he fought and I fired a few arrows into the grey beast. Quaking and exhaling green bile, it fell to the ground. I quickly skinned it and the two others, switching Arnie to manual as we boarded the shuttle.

Approaching the compound the wood and steel walls of our living quarters were ahead, behind them was the large satellite disk and antennae of the Comms centre. The power station was being erected to our right, at the new fence perimeter.

"You there yet?" Stefan's voice interrupted my thoughts, "...need any help?"

"Ah ... sorry mate ... yes I am here, on the West of the planet ... near to a desert area," I replied, keeping a close eye on the construction.

"OK ... I gotta revise again, so how about I teleport two builders to your ship, until you have made the planet your new home-base?" Stefan added helpfully.

"Sounds good, I'll send back the shuttle. Think I'm gonna build The Inn next, so I can transfer crew automatically. Listen up … watch out for giant worms in the desert, just after the mining area," I said, my stomach rumbling. "I'm gonna go eat soon."

Stefan logged off Skype, but in minutes my crew's had two additional workers, which joined the team on the Purple Planet.

"Hey, Marcus," a female voice sounded in my headset, as I returned to my room with ham and cheese sandwiches," how you doin?"

"Hi, Carol … just building my home base … where are you?"

"In the shit on the North side of the planet", she replied, "It's swamp and eats ya health up like crazy."

"Thanks for the warning, hun. Need any help?"

"Think I can manage here", she yawned. God I'm sorry …I'm just soooo tired … will have to pull a sickie tonight. I can do with help on the Ambassador quest; there are two factions on the moon, a Skinhead gang and some religious fanatics. I am unfriendly with both, and can't get through."

"OK, sounds cool … if the skinheads are the Bikers from Alpha Centauri I am friendly with them …

"That figures", she interrupted, giggling.

"… but I know I am hated by the Zealots," I replied, laughing.

"You got plenty of zlots, Commander Petros?" Carol mocked.

"Sure. Enough for both of us. I'll shuttle back to the ship, leaving Arnie down here on "Auto-protect". We can take Language Expert …my robot."

"Who is Arnie, when he's at home?" she quipped. "You didn't buy the Special Edition did you? … you idiot - in two months BlizzCom will patch the name change anyway."

"I know that, Princess Leila, but now I have extra welly in hyper-drive." I replied defensively.

"See you on the Purple Planet's moon ... ya can't miss it ... great big ball in the sky."

Carol logged off Skype. We went to escort an Ambassador, and save an Earthling: All in a day's work as a Star Commander.

Chapter 22 Lectures In The Underworld

A senior demon gathered his class together in his Underworld cavern and gave them his lecture of Induction. His bony finger pointed to his pupils menacingly.

"Soon you will be sent up to the earth above to torment and worry the humans. Above every duty that you have is that of deception. You must spread lies and mischiefs about you know who."

"About who, Master?" a small red imp voiced.

Nudging him hard in the back another imp snarled, "Shut up you dope!"

"But lies about whom?" whimpered the first imp, rubbing his bruised back.

The senior demon, curling his evil lips said, "The maker, creator, Supreme Being etc. etc. I have given you notes to counter arguments which prove His existence. Let's go through them.

"The first argument humans will have is the Argument from Reason. This is called The Ontological Argument, and is attributed to St. Anselm, and latterly by Descartes. Put simply it states that "if we can conceive the concept of God, it is no longer logical to accept that He doesn't exist". If we have the idea of a Perfect Being, we must ask logically where that idea sprung from if it has no logic."

"But we know He exists," the small imp questioned. It was the last thing he did, as a fiery bolt from the senior demon turned him into a pillar of flames.

All that remained was a charred and smoking heap of ash.

"Secondly is the argument from Design, or The Teleological Argument. If there is any proof of order or design in the Universe, it implies a Designer. As the design includes personality, intelligence, reason, morals, conscience, it must be that the Designer has similar characteristics, that a Person with a Mind and Will made the worlds. Consider for design, that the tiniest structure of electrons and nucleus, is identical to the largest structure of Sun and planets. Look at the incredible design in nature, for example the human eye, ear, lungs, and imagine anything compatible made by man."

A large green demon spoke up with, "what can we use, Master, to counter these arguments?"

"I will give you additional notes after this Induction, but basically sow doubts by suggesting that logic sometimes misleads and though there is design there are also flaws in the Universe. Try to get humans to argue amongst themselves about their beliefs, even cause wars if you can! In the Middle Ages we inspired theologians to argue about how many angels could stand on a pin-head!"

There were loud guffaws and titters at that statement.

"But didn't our father cause those flaws, Master, when he fell to Earth?"

"BE QUIET! It is irrelevant where the flaws come from. Our job is to whisper to human ears that there is suffering, chaos and imperfection in the world, and blame the design. GOT IT?"

"Yes, Master!" all the imps, goblins and demons echoed with fear.

"Right, the next argument is The Moral Argument. Humans have and accept moral laws, and acknowledge authority. Why allow command and laws, why accept codes of behaviour? The logic is, that conscience and laws have been "given" rather than made by mankind. Therefore a Moral Being exists."

"Master," an imp groveled, "please indulge a question. What is our answer to this argument?"

"Simply put, we tempt humans to break the laws, defile their consciences. Once they are trapped we entice them into feeling resentment against the laws and Lawgiver. Our job is to entice humans to believe that the laws are unfair, the Lawgiver unjust, and does not exist after all."

"Good one, Master," a demon proclaimed.

"Fourthly is The Argument of First Cause. At some point the Universe came into being, it is an Effect. Nothing comes from nothing. This argues that only a Being outside of time and space could cause the effect.

Finally today, though, of course, there are many others, is The Anthropological Argument. This is based on Man. Man is so intricately made and yet has a "God-shaped void" in his centre. Wherever we travel we find man has a "soul" and makes attempts to worship. Where does this spiritual ache come from?"

"What do we suggest to humans about these arguments?"

"First cause is not easy. I would simply spread the lie that the Universe is The Cause. If anyone asks how that can be, suggest a Big Bang. Humans love mystery. Man's innate desire to worship is a huge source of fun for us. We give humans lots of things to worship But whatever you do, DO NOT MENTION THE SOUL."

"Forgive my interruption again, Master. Is there not a large argument based on The Nazarene?" Hurrying across the classroom to strike the questioning pupil the Master frowned.

"That name and person must not be mentioned. It's true that His life is the most damaging to our lies. Humans are fickle, though, and did kill Him. So let's not worry."

"But didn't He rise again and come down here and take away The Keys of Death and Hell from our Lord?" a quivering voice asked.

Glowing yellow and red with anger the senior demon choked and roared, "LIES. IT'S ALL LIES. Now go and torment, confuse and deceive. Remember God does not exist, and by the way, neither do we, so be careful".

Chapter 23 Havoc At Church

"Being without a pastor is a real pain", Peter said to the Church Board. "It probably costs us as much to pay visiting speakers at every service, as it would to pay a Minister. I don't know about you guys, but I am run ragged, trying to do all the calls". Stroking his hair with his hand, and wiping his brow, he made notes on an A4 pad.

"Pete is right", Marty said, "old Mrs. Harris is in hospital again, and her family are saying she hasn't had a visit."

"We can't do everything", Tom said. "Anyway, she was visited last time. Why don't her family get off their arses (pardon my French), and do something?" He looked at the other two to gauge their response.

"I'd like us to vote on applying to The District for a list of potential pastors" leaning back in a plastic chair, Peter said, taking a note of his suggestion in the Minutes.

"I'll go along with that," Tom said, "just as long as we can invite some who are leading churches. We don't want someone like last time: retired and looking for a hand-out." Tom stroked his greying beard.

"Are we all in favour then?" Peter said. "Marty are you on board?" The other two nodded and Peter took down an official note. The meeting had only taken twenty minutes. He thought, *"I can be home to watch Eastenders."*

Arriving home just before eight, Peter checked phone messages on his answering machine, and sat down in a recliner settee in the lounge and switched on the TV. Hearing him come in, his wife called from upstairs.

"That you, Pete?"

Thinking to himself, *"well if I'm "the mad-axe man", I'm not gonna say, am I?"*

"Yes, sweetheart, it's me," he called back, cupping his mouth with his hands, to be heard over the TV.

He heard Megan treading down the stairs gently, and opening the lounge door. Seeing her pregnant form he felt a glow inside. She kissed him on the cheek, sitting down beside him with a bump. Taking his A4 notepad he showed her the minutes of the meeting.

"Susan sleeping?" he asked.

"Hope so, by now," Megan said, yawning.

Between the soaps Peter outlined his plan, to call The District, and schedule prospects into the church calendar.

"Sounds good, babe" Megan said, yawning again and thumping him on the arm. "I'm knackered. Gonna hit the sack."

Peter pulled the Church Directory from a kitchen drawer and made a note of the numbers to call. He thought: "*I'll also call John; he may know someone who is looking for a church.*"

At the next monthly Deacons' meeting Peter placed papers in front of the other Board members. Marty picked up the paper like it was gold-dust. Tom drew happy or sad faces alongside the names and phone numbers. The District Superintendent had suggested four names, two without churches, two incumbent. Next to the name there was a brief Bio.

"Unless there are any objections", Peter said," I'd like to call these guys and arrange a few preaching Sundays. I suggest we schedule over four months, one a month, and use our monthly Visitor's Sunday, so the folk can get to know them over tea and biscuits."

"Sounds cool," Marty said. The newest member of the Church Board shuffled in his chair. At first he had been uncomfortable with Tom, who seemed crude and abrupt, but Marty had grown to respect him.

"I may be lambing, but I'll make it when I can," Tom said, dusting hay off his jeans. "Won't Megan be dropping hers in May as well?" The farmer sat back, relaxed with his two friends.

"We can work around all our commitments," Peter said, giving Tom a wink. "I'll make the contact and we can announce on Sunday what we are doing." Making a note in his Filofax, he looked at the nodding heads.

The first prospect preached well at the Morning Service. Staying with Marty's mum for dinner, he seemed at home tucking into Roast Beef and Yorkshire pudding. Dishing out a Lemon Cheesecake Dessert, she beamed with exuberance. Her husband, not a church attender, refrained from burping or farting at the table, and had kept to the promised two pints at his local.

The Visitor's service was average, according to The Harris family, who made their views known over refreshments. Showing discontent that the plates only contained biscuits, they made a bee-line for Megan. After a heated exchange, witnessed by the visiting speaker, it was apparent he was not impressed when Tom intervened with: "Piss off. Bring your own food next time."

Peter walked on egg-shells at the next Board meeting, as he produced a letter from the candidate.

"Dear Sirs,

Having thought seriously about your vacancy, I have decided to decline. In fact, I have removed my name from the Prospects List, my current congregation, whilst not as large as yours, are quite a content group.

I wish you all the best in your search.

Yours, etc.

"Cheeky bugger," Tom said. "I bet they've offered him more money."

"Mum liked him," Marty said, "not sure dad did."

"Aye, next time let your dad take them to the Swan," Tom suggested. He left the room singing:
"Four green clergy, hanging on a wall…four green clergy, hanging on a wall…."

The second prospect was a total disaster. Hands shaking at the Communion table, he had popped to the loo, and left his trouser fly undone. Mavis, the Organist had noticed, blushed, and pointed to his zip, making coughing noises. The poor man quickly turned his back, zipped up his fly, but when he turned to face the church, he had inadvertently zipped up the communion cloth too.

The white cloth was tugged, communion glasses spilling on the floor, the metal dishes with bread loaves careering up the aisle. There was pandemonium and havoc in the church.

Mavis chuckled at the Organ and could not play another hymn. Tom laughed so loud he started everyone, until the whole congregation roared. The preacher tried his best with his sermon, but by then the church was too engrossed in frivolity. At the end of the service Peter approached him, shook his hand, and took him for a quiet word in the vestry.

As the guest drove away, Peter was announcing that it was decided they should hold an informal service that evening with no speaker. People shared their own stories, some youngsters sang, and the church had the best time ever! As Tom was busy lambing, and Marty was away with his IT job, Peter met with them briefly over coffee, suggesting that they meet after the next speaker, the following month.

The third visiting preacher was not pastoring when the dates were arranged, but he had mentioned over the phone that he had a number of invitations. Peter placed the phone down strongly, and told Megan the outcome.

"He must think he's God's gift," Peter said," He wants us to make a quick decision."

"That doesn't sound right to me," Megan replied. "Does he really want to come here or not?"

The third guest speaker was a fifty year old, immaculately dressed in a dark blue suit, crisp-white shirt and striped tie. In his breast pocket he had a handkerchief, which he used profusely in his messages, as he preached up a storm. His sermons were superbly crafted, alliterated and complete with illustrations. His messages, appearing to delight the Harris family, were so deep it was difficult to grasp the point.

Whilst he moved smoothly, greeting members of the congregation, his eyes went to and fro, when he talked with anyone. Peter watched with some dread, and also some happiness, when Tom sat next to the man. The man stood up after a heated exchange, banging his coffee down. Peter walked over to Tom, the guest speaker making his way to the vestry for his case.

"What on earth did you say to him, Tom?" Peter inquired, half smiling.

"I told that wind-bag I had read that sermon in Spurgeon's sermons, and even heard a Baptist preach it," Tom said. "The man is a fake; a performer, not the kind we need here." Marty and his mum joined the twosome, both affirming that they didn't trust the man.

"Okay, that's it then," Peter said, "Three down, one to go!"

Late on Sunday evening, the phone rang; Peter pulled his dressing-gown chord and said, "Hello". He called Megan, who ambled into the hall-way. "You will never believe it. He has run off with his Organist."

"Who has?" Megan said, rubbing his eyes and stretching her back, feeling the weight of her baby inside her.

"The guy who has just preached, you ninny," Peter said with an air of smugness, bursting to tell Tom and Marty.

Within a week Megan went into labour, and the couple rejoiced in the birth of a healthy baby girl.

"I'll be outnumbered now," Peter said, "with you, Susan and another female." As he looked into the cot, the infant cried, backing up his fears. "She looks a lot like your mum".

The final guest speaker was a young man, freshly graduated. During the morning service the whole Harris family stormed out, slamming the door. The preacher shrugged his shoulders at Peter.

Tom called out, "Carry on mate, carry on, we're better without them bu…bu..buzzards." he stuttered. The church relieved that Tom has suppressed his profanity. In one prayer meeting he had prayed aloud, "Lord give us the milk of your Word; we're tired of drinking at the Runt tit." One family stormed out and never came back, offended at what they regarded as "coarse language". Peter smiled, thinking "maybe he should have said teat?"

Over washing up the dinner dishes with Marty and his mother, the visitor asked if he could walk around the town. Surprised, they agreed, and went with him. Marty knocked his mother on the shoulder, as the young preacher sat on a bench next to some skin-headed youngsters. They engaged in discussion for some time, followed by the preacher praying with them. Marty and his mum held their hands to their mouths. In Marty's house the preacher talked on the settee with Marty's dad, who nodded and laughed.

At the evening Guest service, three young people, new to the church, sat on the front row, their red and blue spiked hair causing whispers. The preacher welcomed them, and announced that anyone could stay afterwards for coffee. Taking a puppet from his brief case, the children, called to the front, were told a story. Parents, even Marty's dad, clapped at the end.

Holding the new-born in his arms, he and Megan deep in conversation, Peter, Tom and Marty joined them.

"We would like you to become our Pastor," the Board said.

"Thank you very much," the young man said. "Does it matter that I'm having a sex-change?"

The Board choked and spluttered, looking at each other, and at him and Megan.

He and Megan roared with laughter," only joking," he said. "But we must be open to all, equality and diversity must apply to any church I lead.

"The bugger," said Tom, "I like him."

Three months later at a baptismal service, the new minister plunged ten new members into the water. Filling six water-pistols, and handing them to several children, he invited a cowboy shoot-out. There was havoc in the church, for the second time, as people got soaked, but it was great fun.

Chapter 24 The Bench Saw It All

A lonely bench in the isolated park invited occupants. The moonlight lit up its eerie existence. The cold wooden structure was waiting for anyone to come.

Andrew picked up another Burger King French fry, "She won't come, and I just know she won't."

Looking towards his friend John replied, "She is out of your league mate, I wouldn't worry."

Wistfully Andrew placed the remnants of his chicken between his lips, was about to say something, but clammed up. Andrew Jameson, a shy eighteen year old data-entry clerk, was not good with words. Real life conversations made him nervous.

Assuming his friend John had his interests at heart Andrew dropped the empty box and papers into the bin and walked back to the offices of Ansvar Insurance.

From a distance he could see Zarah working near to the Xerox machine. The way she moved tantalised every male within spitting distance, and probably a few females. Her perfectly formed body, the face of a goddess, shoulder-length blond hair and an intoxicating smile. She was everything Andrew wanted in a girl-friend or even one date.

The previous day, after weeks of torment, Andrew had finally plucked up the courage to strike up a conversation.

"Hi, I am Andrew"

"Oh, hello," she flashed her heart-melting smile.

"How are you settling in?" was Andrew's opener.

"Okay I guess. I think so anyway. You're in data-entry, right?" she inquired raising her eyebrows.

Andrew found it impossible not to stare at her cleavage as he raised his eyes towards her, "Yeah." End of conversation.

As John waited for his friend a few weeks ago he had noticed the new girl coming out of Ansvar's building. "My have we here?" he muttered under his breath, "What a babe!" Approaching the hurrying form John called out, "Wait a minute, can we share a taxi?" At that second he didn't spare a thought for his friend who would descend the stone steps in minutes.
"Sorry, I am taking the bus", Zarah shyly answered. Something about the guy made her nervous, so she had lied.
"Okay, maybe another time."
Zarah walked on towards the bus-stop. Happy that she was out of sight, she called a taxi, giving a curious destination for someone appearing so young.
As they walked home that evening John grew bored with his friend's ranting about the new girl in the office. One important fact was divulged, her name was Zarah. Attempting to feign interest John prompted the data-entry clerk to disclose more.
"She moved from L & G, and is now assisting us with Compliance. I am thinking of asking her out," Andrew looked towards his friend for approval of his plan.
"It's up to you, mate. But she sounds like a real ball-breaker. Are you sure you want to get egg on your face?"
"Maybe not then,"a deflated Andrew walked on.

Andrew knew he had failed at his life and relationships, as he gazed at Zarah from a distance, trying to think of another way to approach her. "Coffee, why not coffee?" he reasoned. Leaving his desk, nodding to his team supervisor, indicating with hand signals a coffee-break, Andrew made his way to the machine.

Searching out Zarah he approached her, taking a deep breath.

"Would you like a drink, Zarah?" His future hopes were in the next sentence.

"Ooh, yes please, do they have Cadbury hot chocolate?" she asked innocently, knowing full well that they did.

"Yes. I will get you one."

"Meet me in the canteen, I hate drinking at my work-station, it's unprofessional."

"Okay" a jubilant Andrew hurried to the drinks machine, making a note to never drink at his work-station.

The next fifteen minutes were some of the happiest moments the teenager had enjoyed. It was like Christmas as a toddler, all his emotional fairy-lights were lit. He could not believe his luck when she agreed to meet him in the park after work the next day. Partially running, part skipping, an elated junior clerk made his way up The Boulevard in Cheltenham. The home of insurance giants.

"It could be him," Zarah,- real name DC Joanne Burton- said, "the girls have all worked in Insurance, and Ansvar has not been hit yet." Joanne was an under-cover officer with Serious Crimes. She was on a team in Cheltenham investigating a series of sexual assaults on young office workers. Andrew was in her sights.

"I'm not sure, if it is him as he seems quite shy. I have arranged a meeting tomorrow in an isolated spot."

"Okay," the DCI in charge of the investigation code-named "INDIGO" for "Insurance girl", "We will wire you and have officers in situ around the park. Be careful," he cautioned.

Following the lunch at Burger King it took Andrew most of the afternoon to rise from the gut-feeling of gloom. Should he cancel the meeting, to save embarrassment? Watching Zarah, catching her eyes several time, he tried to assess whether she was a tease or going to be a "no-show". Since he reached his teens he had experienced the agony of waiting in a cafe or cinema queue with his date not appearing. He felt trepidation that it could happen. Willing to take the risk he approached Zarah.

"We still on for tonight?" butterflies in his stomach.
"Okay, that'll be good. See ya in the park about 5.30. I will be on the bench near the entrance."
"Great," Andrew stated, too enthusiastically.
Prior to leaving the offices at 5 he popped into the gents to spray on some Lynx deodorant. Checking his appearance in the mirror he combed his fingers through his hair and sucked in his stomach.
Descending the steps he noticed John waiting, looking perturbed.
"Sorry mate, she can't come. She just flew past me in a rush. Some sort of family crisis." John was an adept liar. He had used his skill four times up to that night, luring office workers to lonely spots.

"How do you know her?" a puzzled Andrew inquired. "Yesterday you said she was out of my league. When have you seen her?"

"Listen, mate, if you don't believe me, that's fine. Just turn up and see. Be Johnny-no-mates. Reason I know it's her as she must have seen us meet and introduced herself. But you go if you want to. I only came to warn you."

A depressed and torn Andrew saw his friend walk away. It appeared life had dealt him a rotten hand once again. He decided that he would go to the park anyway.

John stood Standing in the dark and saw the attractive Compliance officer come through the park gates. It was 5.15pm. As she passed he lunged at her, grabbing her shoulders, forcing her to the ground behind a bush.

"Your little boy-friend is not coming, you cock-tease. But I will give you some action." Holding a commando-knife inches from her face he menaced, "Make a sound and I will stick you with this."

Suddenly for John it all went very wrong. The office worker twisted and kneed him between his legs, grabbing him she man-handling him onto the floor. Flipping him onto his back she cuffed him.

Thinking her back-up had arrived as the bushes parted she was surprised at the appearance out of the dark of her date. Andrew took in the scene immediately and sat on John's squirming back. Secretly he knew his so-called friend was an ass-hole.
"I am so sorry, "Andrew filled up with tears. "How could he?"

Her real back-up arrived.

"John Sparkes I am arresting you on suspicion of attempted sexual assault and threatening with a weapon. You have the right to remain silent. You have the right to a lawyer. Anything you say will be taken down and may be used in evidence. Do you understand your rights?"

"Yeah, whatever, you bitch."

Some days later after completing a statement Andrew the data-entry clerk was formerly introduced to DC Joanne Burton, a married twenty-eight year old under-cover officer. Disappointed that she would never be his date he took encouragement from his new-found popularity in the office. Someone at the police station had leaked his involvement, hailing him a have-a-go hero. A new girl in the Compliance Office dropped him an e-mail invited him to her sixteenth birthday party.
She had seen his picture in The Gloucestershire News and thought he was "cool!"

The park bench was alone in the moonlight, but not for long.

Chapter 25 Stuck In An Elevator

Pulling my Ford Focus into a space, I turned to my passenger and said, "we OK to have a bite before the meeting?"

"Yes, of course," Brian replied, "but nothing fancy." I chuckled.

The Board of the Housing Association served basic sandwiches of ham, cheese, tuna and salad with a few crisps. It was never 'fancy' but I suppose my tastes were used to the pickle or mayonnaise. The committee meeting always started on time at 6pm, as I was the Chair, so thirty minutes tops for a bite in the plush staff-room.

The agenda went well, with no absentees or serious questions. Once again I had tried to steer to the committee to a sound and worthwhile conclusion. The minutes would reflect the views of the group. It was time to go home.

"Have you got a minute?" the Chief Executive asked. I always found Mike to be open and straight, so signalled to Brian that he could catch a ride with another member. After fifteen minutes I understood Mike's proposals and agreed to think it all through and get back to him. I was about to call Meg, my wife, when I realised my Nokia phone was on the bedside cabinet charging. "Oh, well," I thought, "I won't be much longer", which was the reason I took the lift instead of the stairs.

At 7.30pm on Friday evening I pressed the Down arrow and waited. The sound of others on the stairs and cleaners' vacuuming gave me a feeling of hurry: it really was time to go home. The solid metal lift doors opened with a 'SWISH' and I entered. Though Meg had problems with lifts and moving stairs I was OK with them. On the console I pressed "G" and the mechanism started. As we moved downwards I checked myself in the mirror. Soon I would be heading home.

The first moment I realised something was wrong was the smell. Metal, rubber, bearings, whatever was emitting a horrid stink. There was no smoke, but suddenly the lift shuddered and stopped. The lovely ladies voice did not say, "doors opening" and it went quiet. I checked my watch: "half-way through Corrie" I thought. The neon lights shone in the chamber, so I calmly (or maybe not so calmly), read what to do. "Is it an Emergency?" I thought, "I guess so, the bloody thing is stuck." So I pulled the red lever. I immediately thought of "Die Hard" and wondered if I could be Bruce Willis. I didn't have a vest.

I waited. No sounds were on the stairs; cleaners all gone home. "Aye, home watching Corrie I bet," I thought. It was eerie but since the grinding noises there was no strong smell. I was relieved there was no smoke. "FIRE: Do not use the lift, use the stairs." Yep I was glad there was no smoke. I began to wonder things like: how will the Emergency guys get into the building? Will they use acetylene on the lift doors? Will I hear them coming? Just to make sure I shouted out, "IN HERE", and decided I would do that very loudly if I saw sparks on the doors. Then I wondered about any damage. "OH bugger," I said to myself, "this could cost us an arm and a leg; think of the cuts!" I decided I might as well sit down.

On the cold hard lift floor I waited. It started to get cold in the lift. I wondered about oxygen and other things; like how long can I live without water and what if I need a pee before help comes? It took ninety minutes for help to come. The red Emergency was linked to the lift operator call-out not the fire-brigade. Ninety minutes sitting on a cold floor in my new suit! There was no smashing of glass in the main doors: they used a master-key. There was not the sound of hunky firemen on the stairs, merely the breathless panting of one older guy. He was probably as old as me.

A metal lever appeared forcing opens the doors: a bit like the jemmy burglars' use. "God", I thought," what does he do at weekends?"

Anyway, Ron, as that was his name, was OK. Once the doors were "jemmied" open he dropped into the lift carriage and inserted a key into the console. The lights blinked and we started to move. "MIND THE DOORS" the voice said: Too bloody right!

Chapter 26 A Photo Shock

Sometimes my photo expertise has been questioned. Rabbits with red eyes, my dad with his head missing, a hand at the edge of some beach scenes. Our album is a great example of how NOT to take photos. "A bad workman blames his tools," my mother would say, so I can't blame the camera. With the digital era it should all be much easier,"PRESS, FLASH,SAVE AND PRINT." It's not true that all my snaps are bad: I've given a few laughs at Christmas.

"It's about time you took some photos with our heads on," my wife joked.

My wife's sister Anne said, "Don't be hard on him. He needs practice." She winked.

Some days later I took a call from Anne which made my day. "Would you like to help our Nell with her media project?" Anne said.

"Err, yes, of course I will help. What does she need?" I replied into the phone.

"She wants you to take some photos," she said. My wife was not at home, but I could imagine her laughter.

I arranged to meet Nell over coffee the next day. She explained exactly what she wanted.

"You're not pulling my leg? Is it a kind of Before and After of photoing?" I asked.

No, it's OK, honest. I've screwed up on the "at home with nature shots" and need some help. The project must be handed in next week," she said, her eyes pleading. So I arranged a photo-shoot for the next day; in our local park. The park was an ideal nature setting with plenty of grass and tress. It was large enough for us to pose without disturbance.

It was a sunny day, though there was a bit of mist near the trees. She had chosen a white smock of cotton, which accentuated her shape and looked almost innocent. The dress was quite bridal. With her bare legs in my phone camera's view-finder I thought she looked virginal and reminded me of a shampoo advert on the TV. I could imagine her dancing through the hay-field chewing buttercups. The sunshine made her dress glow.

I noticed Nell was looking weary. All the posing and my "direction" had proved a bit taxing so I said, "OK Nell, why not sit on the grass and take a rest?" With Nell dozing I took a few snaps and decided I would check them when I got home.

At home I plugged my phone into my PC via the USB cable and started to view the pictures. I scrolled image to image, deleting the ones with Nell's face blurred or her looking the wrong way. As I reached the last few photos I went cold. Nell was lying asleep on the grass and over her was a ghost-like apparition. The figure had a sharp contrast to natural surroundings. It was almost ethereal and transparent, towering over Nell like a protector. Nell lay on the soft green grass, her white dress revealing her innocent pose. Over her with arms akimbo is a translucent figure. At first I thought it was a mistake of the camera: it was like a negative image, the facial features grey/black and the hair white. The eyes of the phantom were penetratingly white.

I printed Nell's photos and gave them to her, but did not include the last three. In the town library some days later I browsed through any reports of ghosts seen in the park, but I drew a blank. I have since searched the internet for "ghostly sitings" in the UK. Ghosts in pubs, appearances in libraries, factories, stately homes. Fascinating groups exist who believe in the 'paranormal'; some being total nutters, but there are some genuine researchers. Reading of a priest who specialises in the phenomena I arranged to travel up the motorway to hear of his experiences.

"Most appearances are displaced humans. They're not malicious," he stated matter-of-factly as we sat in the Service Area. "If there is a family link the ghost is attempting communication." I was glad to know my niece was not in danger.

The photo of Nell and her supernatural guardian has remained a mystery. I did not tell Nell; in fact I have shared this with only one other person.. You are the first.

Chapter 27 In The Dark

One of my favourite films is "The Scent of a Woman." If you have never watched it I can heartily recommend it: Al Pacino is brilliant and believable as a blind ex. Lieutenant Colonel who needs a chaperone. As the tale develops we find the colonel is a wonderful Tango dancer; even as a blind person! I won't spoil your enjoyment by telling you the scenes at the Public School are classic. What I most remember from the film is the colonel's frustrated anger with the phrase, "I'm in the dark here!" Well worth the watch.

I very recently bought a new car; a brand new Ford Focus. The dealer sold me on the idea of using the "automatic lighting" feature. It works well at night time: my lights are brilliant beams. In fog, however, I am in the dark and cant find where the light control is!

Being in the dark is an experience that can affect us all, young and old; physical or spiritual. Sometimes we need someone to "turn on the light".
My nephew was born visually impaired, and by the time he was four of five he was totally blind. His impairment did not deter him from riding a push-bike, getting a job or moving into his own apartment. Andrew is still an amazing example of a human being.

When I was a toddler my grandparents had a farm. In the UK we would call it a 'small holding' as there was no livestock except chickens. I have so many happy memories of life there. Apparently I was "farmed out" (see the play on words?) to my grandad Fred and grandma Nellie over school holidays. I like to believe that this wasn't because I was mischievous, but rather because I had two older brothers. Three lads over the summer was a huge challenge.

As I said, I have many happy memories which I will recall, but first I want to tell of one not so pleasant. My mum and dad were helping - on this occasion - to dip flowers in coloured dye. My brothers were running wild somewhere so I was placed in a "skip." Now before you get all hot and bothered and call Child Protection, it was not a "skip" as we know today: with metal sides and dumped on a drive. This skip was a large wicker basket. The idea was that I was too small to climb out, the weight kept it solidly placed, so I was in a kind of "play pen".

What nobody realised was that as I struggled and jumped, the lid closed. I was in the dark. I remember being scared; I think for the first time in my life. Some splits in the construction made a few air and light holes, but it was really dark. I cried but was unheard as everyone was further away collecting more flowers to colour. For ages I was afraid, alone, and in the dark. Fortunately for me my dad noticed my predicament and rescued me. I have sold memories of being lifted and held. The sun's rays were dazzling; the sky more blue. I have never since been afraid of the dark.

My time in that skip was the only bad experience I had on the farm, unless scratches count, and some hens that pecked. I had chores and could explore when I wasn't needed. As I got older I became a pirate, a soldier, Robin Hood and Huckleberry Finn. The sights and sounds of farm life were thrilling throughout my childhood. Apart from gathering peas, which was my favourite assignment, I also collected eggs daily. My grandma insisted I "whistle" when pea harvesting as I love raw peas and there would be none to sell if I ate them all. Eggs, however, were different. It was a daily treasure hunt to find them. The crafty layers had hid them in the grass, under bushes, and in corners of the hen house. Some still sat on them refusing to surrender them. My grandad called them "broody". I also had to feed the chickens. The store was a wooden shed with two huge bins inside. One bin held oats, the other corn, easily placed in a bucket buy scooping it out.

I was not scared of any rats as my grandma's terrier called "Gypsy" sorted them out within seconds!

Another job I really liked was cutting lettuces and washing them in a tin bath. I don't know what it is about boys and water, but a hosepipe is a million times better than a water pistol. Spray would splash everywhere, sometimes accidentally reach "Gypsy" who would yap and drink it; her jaws and tongue flapping. The lettuces would be gently placed in cardboard boxes, twenty four at a time, ready for market. In my grandad's van were placed buckets of dyed flowers, boxes of lettuce and tomatoes and cartons of eggs.

Market days in Sandbach and Holmes Chapel were buzzing in those days. I loved being a salesman, taking customers money and giving change. I have always been pretty good at mental arithmetic so could work prices out in my head. The cash box was overflowing with coins; in those days they were halfpennies, pennies, shillings, and silver pieces. In our cash tin were "ten bob notes", pound notes were rare, and five pound notes even rarer. On market day in Holmes Chapel there was livestock auctions. Whilst I did not attend any of the sales times I was allowed to wander and see animals in their pens. Cows, sheep and pigs brought the real "farmyard smells".

When my family joined me at the farm there were wonderful outings. On Sundays evenings we went to "The Black Swan" at Arclid; which my dad called "The Mucky Duck". Arclid was a weird place for me as a boy as the local mental hospital had an 'open door policy'. The patients scared me: but I am a lot older now, and wiser. At The Black Swan the children had crisps (potato chips) and bottles of Tizer while dad had a pint and mum had a Mackeson. There were also swings and bowls on the Green. I didn't try it.

Another family outing was to the banks of the River Dane at Radnor bank. One of the earliest photos of me is of me just peeping over the river bank into the camera. Once again I was a toddler; too small to climb out. My two brothers splashed and swam in the rivers swirling cold waters. When I was older I would join the fun: sliding down the sandbanks and jumping into the freezing water. Making damns was our serious and industrious activity. Stone, rocks, branches and mud were carefully constructed together in the water. Our labours often produced a sizeable obstacle, often creating a deep lake. It was deep to us boys anyway. Making things on water became my occupation much later as my friends and I built rafts of oil drums and doors. I became Huckleberry Finn again on the canal near my home.

Life on the farm was rewarding at "potato harvest" times as -, when I was old enough - I joined the potato pickers and pocketed a handy ten shillings a day. My wages were spent on comics and sweets. I remember as a youngster reading Beano and Dandy. Later my tastes would change and the comics were Superman and Batman. Reading was a big part of my life. I loved the Tarzan books my Edgar Rice Burrows. As a very small child my mum had read stories of a rabbit; I think it was called Brere or something.

As well as reading books I was a passionate "I-Spy fan". I bought the books from WH Smith (no Amazon then) and diligently pursued the books' contents for animals, birds, insects and trees. I have introduced my grand-children to the world of I-Spy books recently. My friend's mum had the Daily Mail. My friends and I sat together translating coded messages from "Big Chief I-Spy and I got a feather for doing so. It was pretty easy on the farm to find birds and insects. My dad had a pet fox and crow when he was a boy. Now we have dogs.

I guess my memoirs of the farm should include my dad collecting tomatoes from the four massive greenhouses. As he was colour-blind my dad picked unripe green fruit. I asked him once what he did at traffic lights. He replied that he knew where the various signals were, irrespective of colour. Driving was very important to my dad. He was a patrolman with The Automobile Association, and his job depended on his driving. He talked a lot about his job, but never about the war.

Farm life was exciting for me as a lad. There were no tractors or machinery; apart from a diesel driven rotating plough. My memories bring joy to my mind. I try to pass them on to my family. We should keep them alive and live as innocently as we did as children.

Prologue Of The Eden Tree

I was here. I had taken the decision to follow my destiny. Made plans and left my home and family. Now I was alone in a strange place. I could endure the foreign climate and customs if the stranger had what he promised. It had been a long journey, but I was not following a star: I was pursuing a box.

On my own except for the taxi driver who slotted the gear in Drive and moved the green and white Volvo forwards. My body jerked to right and left as the taxi moved in the traffic. Bright lights from the windows of the airport arrivals appeared behind. Cars honked as we manoeuvred unsteadily, bright neon lights cast shadows across our path. Alien sights passed me through misted windows.

The city of Tel Aviv -- modern Jaffa - was a major tourist destination known as "The City that never sleeps". Monday evening's taxi ride from Ben-union International airport -about 12 miles outside of the metropolitan area- was a scenic manifestation of man's creations ancient and modern. Steel structures reached towards the moon, rectangles of light interrupting their shiny exteriors. Stone edifices lit up with subtle glows from lights placed at their bases. Green, orange and white beams illuminated tourist attractions. Vaguely discernable red and white striped market stalls, cardboard moved to a gentle breeze. Remnants of the day's activity.

The taxi braked suddenly; my body thrown against the rear passenger door. "Sorry, Sir," the bearded driver said over his shoulder, "the other drivers do not observe my signals." His accent was guttural, probably Arabic, his pronunciation staggered.

Scanning the flapping identity card attached to the steering column by a black cord, I said: "that's okay, ... Ahmed. We're in no hurry."

I hoped he got my subtle hint. Fate had carried me aloft with strong arms to leave my home and family. I had crossed the globe to fulfil my destiny; not to become a road-traffic casualty. White smoke trailed from a car in front

My body realised we were circling a huge roundabout.
"This is our harbour, Sir," the driver spoke again. "Over four thousand years she remains. Much blood has been shed."
The tranquil night-time scenes drew a veil over centuries of war. My spine tingling, I knew I faced my own conflict.

My finger-tips felt the chilly wetness as I wiped the misted windows. Orange-tinted night-light from street lamps gave an eerie glow. My nose pressed against the cold glass. I could make out the Mediterranean lapping gently against the steps of the stone esplanade like probing wet fingers. A mammoth lake of black ink streaked by moonlight. Silvery-white waves splashed against the eroded harbour wall. Well-trodden grey stone steps, snaking to the ocean, looked as old as the hills as we drove by, circumnavigating the old parts of Jaffa. Over his shoulder the taxi driver gave me a potted history. Perhaps he did the same for tourists. I appreciated his effort. He had a job to do.
But I was not here for the tour. My stomach churned. I reached for the photo in my jacket's pocket. Holding it between thumb and finger, I asked myself questions I'd asked on the plane: "Would he be as amiable as his picture portrayed? Did he possess what the brothers claimed? Was the story true? " As we passed an ancient clock tower I looked at my watch.
Holding the passport-sized black and white I gazed at it for the hundredth time. "Was this man part of my destiny?"

I was brought from my thoughts by Ahmed's voice. Through his windscreen I could see tail-lights charting our course as a red-dotted snake.

"Your family, Sir?". He nodded in the rear-view mirror, his eyes falling to the photo.

"Err… no." I hesitated. " It's someone I'm meeting". I replied courteously and returned to my thoughts.

Meeting was the word.

I was miles from home to meet a total stranger. I looked again at my watch, apprehension rising within me, like a petulant toddler demanding attention. Settling into the cloth seat, my thoughts scanned the years like scenes from a movie. The milestones passed to get where we were: comfortably well-off. Our home comforts are acquired by hard relentless endeavour, I reflected. "Is this a plot to con me?"

After a chance meeting at a market these efforts had brought me to Jaffa. Fate, the stars, karma, or a predestined plan, have drawn me to the city like a moth to a flame. Is this my destiny?"

I gave more hurried glances through the window. From the corner of my eye I noticed the Clock Tower again, I breathed a prayer, as the taxi ferried me on. "God, I hope you can help. Time is running out."

Looking again at the photo made my hands clammy. I put it away. Soon I would meet a man who could change our lives forever.

News From The Author

LATEST NEWS

My new novel **"THE EDEN TREE"** is being reviewed currently, and I hope it will be published in 2016.

If you enjoyed the Prologue "Watch This Space".

Meantime most of my writing appears on FanStory. For the link go here:
http://www.fanstory.com/displaystory.jsp?hd=1&id=544572

Made in the USA
Charleston, SC
25 September 2015